# The Nature of Mind

# The Nature of Mind

*The Dzogchen Instructions of Aro Yeshe Jungne*

Patrul Rinpoche

COMMENTARY BY

*Khenchen Palden Sherab*

*and Khenpo Tsewang Dongyal*

Snow Lion
Boulder
2016

Snow Lion
An imprint of Shambhala Publications, Inc.
2129 13th Street
Boulder, Colorado 80302
www.shambhala.com



This book is a revised and updated edition of a book previously published under the title of *Pointing Out the Nature of Mind: Dzogchen Pith Instructions of Aro Yeshe Jungne* (2012).



9 8 7 6 5 4 3

Printed in United States of America

Shambhala Publications makes every effort to print on acid-free, recycled paper.

Snow Lion is distributed worldwide by Penguin Random House, Inc., and its subsidiaries.

Designed by Gopa & Ted2, Inc.

Library of Congress Cataloging-in-Publication Data

Names: O-rgyan-'jigs-med-chos-kyi-dbang-po, Dpal-sprul, 1808–1887, author. | Palden Sherab, Khenchen, 1938–2010. | Tsewang Dongyal, Khenpo, 1950–
Title: The nature of mind: the Dzogchen instructions of Aro Yeshe Jungne / Patrul Rinpoche; commentary by Khenchen Palden Sherab and Khenpo Tsewang Dongyal.
Other titles: Theg mchog a ti'i man ngag gnas lugs gsal ston. English
Description: Boulder: Snow Lion, 2016. | Includes translations from Tibetan.
Identifiers: LCCN 2015019556 | ISBN 9781559394499 (paperback)
Subjects: LCSH: Rdzogs-chen. | Rñiṅ-ma-pa (Sect)—Doctrines. | Ye-shes 'Byung-gnas, A-ro, active 10th century—Teachings. | BISAC: RELIGION / Buddhism / Tibetan. | RELIGION / Buddhism / Sacred Writings.
Classification: LCC BQ7662.4 .O728 2016 | DDC 294.3/444—dc23
LC record available at http://lccn.loc.gov/2015019556

Dedicated in the honor and memory of His Holiness Dudjom Rinpoche,
Venerable Khenchen Palden Sherab Rinpoche, Lama Chimed Namgyal,
and all the lineage holders of these secret teachings,
as well as all the devoted practitioners
of the past, present, and future.

# Contents

# Preface

THE LEGACY OF the enlightened teacher Aro Yeshe Jungne was recently reignited by Khenchen Palden Sherab Rinpoche at Padma Samye Ling, so that these authentic, ever-expanding lineage teachings are now increasing in Western countries as they did in Tibet in the tenth century, near the end of the first millennium C.E.

I had the great fortune and opportunity to join with such a great master as Khenchen Palden Sherab Rinpoche, and am very happy to bring forth this gift of his as a monument of these teachings.

I pray that these teachings will inspire and support practitioners, and that this book honors the great lineage masters and fulfills Khenchen Palden Sherab Rinpoche's wishes, and the wishes of other great masters who entered mahaparinirvana within recent years. I offer this with prayers for their swift reincarnations, which are very much needed during these times.

I also pray that all great lineage masters, world peacemakers, and everyone supporting the cause of peace and harmony have long and healthy lives, fulfill all their wishes, and that all their activities flourish and increase.

I would like to thank everyone who helped with this book, including Richard Steinberg for transcribing and editing all the teachings and creating the glossary, as well as Lama Pema Dragpa, Ann Helm, and Mark Flinton. I would also like to thank Lama Jomo Lorraine and Lama Laia for their ongoing support of the Padmasambhava Buddhist Center.

Holding to the genuine Dharma of the victorious ones,
May we always manifest enlightened deeds;
Perfectly practicing excellent conduct,
May I act in this way throughout all aeons to come.

May the secret teachings of all the victorious ones,
Their incomparably supreme teachings,
Arise as the sun in the sky,
Gloriously pervading the entire universe.

May the lotus feet of the guru who glorifies the teachings be firm.
May the noble ones who hold the teachings encompass the earth.
May the prosperity and dominion of the patrons of the teachings increase.
May the teachings auspiciously remain for a long time.

Bless my mind to turn toward the Dharma.
Bless my Dharma practice to follow the path.
Bless my path to be free of delusion.
Bless me that all delusion be transformed into wisdom.

By realizing true nature, may I mature my own mind.
Through compassion and love, may I mature the minds of others.
May I have meaningful contact with whomever I meet.
May the Lama and the Triple Gem bless me so that this may be fulfilled.

Khenpo Tsewang Dongyal Rinpoche
June 2, 2015
Palden Padma Samye Ling

# Editor's Introduction

Guru Namo. Aro Yeshe Jungne flourished in Tibet in the tenth century. He was a great master and teacher, and the fountainhead of important Dzogchen Mind Section oral transmission lineages within the Nyingma school that thrived for over three centuries. Many people who practiced the Aro teachings became enlightened, and some even attained the transcendental wisdom rainbow body.

In the thirteenth and fourteenth centuries the terma tradition in general and the Dzogchen Essence Instruction Section in particular became increasingly popular in the Nyingma world. Because of this the Aro lineages began to lose momentum and were eventually absorbed into other oral transmission lineages. In the late nineteenth century the great Nyingma master Patrul Rinpoche—thought by some to be a reincarnation of Aro Yeshe Jungne—possibly saved and certainly revitalized the lineage by collecting all the Aro teachings, editing them, and publishing them in a single text. From July 31 to August 6, 2006, the great Nyingma masters Khenchen Palden Sherab Rinpoche and Khenpo Tsewang Dongyal Rinpoche gave extensive teachings on the Aro tradition at their beautiful retreat center, Palden Padma Samye Ling, in Delaware County, New York, thus making them fully available to people of the Western world. The Khenpo Rinpoches' teachings were recorded, edited, and have been published in the form of this book you now hold in your hands.

Aro Yeshe Jungne says look directly into your mind, identify its nature, and abide there. The nature of the mind is open, clear, bright, peaceful, compassionate, complete, and free from thought and emotion. Know this and be this—this is the heart of his message. Aro gives many instructions so this can be accomplished. He arranges these into nine categories, corresponding to the different degrees of readiness and seasoning among human beings to abide in mind-nature. Each one of the teachings in all of the nine categories is a perfect path. Each one of these paths is supported and glorified by cultivating boundless love and compassion, an understanding of impermanence, and devotion, particularly to the root teacher.

The great master Khenchen Palden Sherab Rinpoche left his body on June 19, 2010. He was at once one of the greatest scholars and intellects Tibet has ever produced, and a mahasiddha on par with Sangye Yeshe and Do Khyentse, capable of the most awesome spiritual power, although it seems he chose rarely to display this. He was gentle, humble, kind, generous, and always approachable, as well as being as strong as a lion and utterly mysterious. When Shantarakshita and Atisha each left their homeland in India and arrived in Tibet to live and to teach, their humility and impeccable conduct did not change. The same was true for Khen Rinpoche. He maintained to perfection the three vows—pratimoksha, bodhisattva, and Vajrayana—in the United States just as he did in India and Tibet. To all of us he was an extraordinary, inspiring example of how a Dharma practitioner behaves in this world. He was also omniscient. Whenever you were in his presence it was clear he knew everything about you—and he still loved you! Whatever he said to you, whatever he showed you, was a profound essence instruction spontaneously designed for you, to last a thousand years. Simply to think of him, even now, even for a moment, is to be catapulted into the Dzogchen state. And he knew everything there is to know about Buddhism. I am capable of understanding and communicating only a tiny fraction of his spiritual greatness.

It is with profound gratitude that I dedicate this book to the life, legacy, and swift rebirth of Khenchen Palden Sherab Rinpoche, as well as to the long life and good health of his brother, equally sublime, Khenpo Tsewang Dongyal Rinpoche. May their aspirations be achieved. May everyone everywhere attain complete Dzogchen realization, and enjoy all manner of happiness and prosperity.

I would like to thank Lama Pema Dragpa for his expert technical assistance at every stage of this process, Ann Helm for her impeccable editorial advice, and Mark Flinton for his meticulous work preparing the Aro manuscript for publication. I would also like to thank Sarah Harding for her beautiful translation of the root text by Patrul Rinpoche, Shambhala Publications for their warm support in making this book possible, and Susan Kyser for her wonderful attention to detail and kindness in the final stages of editing.

By this merit may all obtain omniscience;
May it defeat the enemy, wrong-doing.
From the stormy waves of birth, old age, sickness, and death,
From the ocean of samsara, may I free all beings.

May the sole source of benefit and happiness,
The Buddha's teachings, remain for a long time, and
May the victory banner of the lives of the noble ones,
The holders of the teachings, remain firm.

The precious bodhichitta:
In those without it, may it be generated;
In those who have it, may it never diminish,
But always continue increasing.

Sarva Mangalam!

On behalf of the Samye Translation Group
Richard Steinberg (Padma Chodrak)
March 29, 2015
Shantarakshita Library
Palden Padma Samye Ling

# Clear Elucidation of True Nature

*An Esoteric Instruction on the Sublime Approach of Ati*

༄༅ཐེག་མཆོག་ཨ་ཏིའི་མན་ངག་གནས་ལུགས་གསལ་སྟོན་བཞུགས་སོ།[1]

Patrul Rinpoche

Translated by Sarah Harding

བླ་མ་དམ་པ་རྣམས་ལ་ཕྱག་འཚལ་ལོ།

གང་ཟག་དབང་པོ་རབ་འབྲིང་ཐ་མའི་རིམ་པ་གསུམ་སོ་སོ་པས་རང་བཞིན་རྫོགས་པ་ཆེན་པོའི་གནས་ལུགས་སྐྱོང་ཚུལ་ནི། དང་པོ་སེམས་འཚོལ་གྱིས་རིམ་པས་གདར་ཤ་ལེགས་པར་བཅད་ཅིང་བརྗོད་མེད་ཀྱི་དོན་ངོ་ལེགས་པར་འཕྲོད་པ་གཞིར་བཞག་ནས། སྐྱོང་ཚུལ་དངོས་ནི། དབང་པོ་རབ་ཀྱིས་སེམས་ཁོ་རང་གནས་རུང་སེམས་ཡིན། འགྱུ་རུང་སེམས་ཡིན། སེམས་སྟོང་པར་ཐག་ཆོད་ཕྱིན་ཆད་ནས། གནས་འགྱུ་གཉིས་ལ་ཁྱད་པར་ཅི་ཡང་མེད་པས། རྣམ་རྟོག་གང་ཤར་གང་སྣང་ཐམས་ཅད་ཡེ་ཤེས་ཀྱི་རོལ་པ་རྒྱལ་བའི་དགོངས་པ་ཟབ་མོ་སྟོང་པ་ཉིད་ཡིན། དེ་ལ་བཅོས་སླད་གང་ཡང་མ་བྱེད་པར་དེ་ཁའི་ངང་ལ་ཞོག་གནས་སྐབས་སུ་རྣམ་རྟོག་རང་ག་མར་འདུག་ནའང་། ངང་དམ་ཤུགས་ཀྱིས་གྲོལ་ཡོད་པས་ཧིང་འཛིན་ཁོ་ན་ཡིན། ཆོས་སྐུ་ཡིན། རང་བྱུང་གི་ཡེ་ཤེས་ཡིན། ཕྱག་རྒྱ་ཆེན་པོ་ཡིན། ཤེས་རབ་ཀྱི་ཕ་རོལ་ཏུ་ཕྱིན་པ་ཡིན། དཔེ་ཐག་པ་མེས་ཚིག་པ་དང་འདྲ། དེས་འཆིང་མི་ནུས། ཁོ་རང་གི་ངོ་བོ་སྟོང་པ་ཡིན། རྣམ་རྟོག་ལྷར་སྣང་བ་དེ་སྟོང་པའི་གདངས་ཤར་བ་ཡིན། རྣམ་རྟོག་དང་སྟོང་པ་ལ་ཁྱད་པར་མི་འདུག་པས། ཨོ་རྒྱན་ཆེན་པོས། རྣམ་རྟོག་ངོ་བོ་སྟོང་པས་ཆོས་སྐུར་གོ། ཞེས་གསུངས། སྒོམ་ན་བློ་ཡིན་པས་བསྒོམ་རྒྱུ་ཅི་ཡང་མེད། རྣམ་རྟོག་རང་ག་མར་ཞོག་དེ་ལ་བཅས་བཅོས་བྱས་ན་རྣམ་རྟོག་རང་རྒྱུད་པ་འཁྲུལ་པ་ལུ་གུ་རྒྱུད་ཡིན་པས་བཅས་བཅོས་གང་ཡང་མི་བྱ། རང་ཐོག་ཏུ་འཛོག་པ་དེ་ལས་ཡེངས་ན་འཁྲུལ་པ་དངོས་ཡིན་པས་མ་

Homage to all genuine gurus.

THIS IS THE WAY to cultivate the true nature in the natural great completion according to three specific processes for persons of best, average, and lesser capabilities. The foundation is laid by receiving the proper introduction to the nature of the ineffable, having first applied finely honed discernment in the process of searching for the mind. The actual way to cultivate it is as follows.

## Best Capability

For a person of best capability, mind itself is mind when it is still and it is mind when it moves. Once you are convinced that mind is empty, there is no difference at all between stillness and movement. Whatever thoughts arise, whatever appears, is all the play of pristine wisdom. This is the emptiness that is the profound perspective of all victorious ones. Rest within that itself without adulterating it in any way. Although occasionally there are regular thoughts, since they are liberated automatically or within that state, it is only meditative absorption. It is dharmakaya. It is innately occurring pristine wisdom. It is the Great Seal (Mahamudra). It is the perfection of transcendent intelligence (Prajnaparamita). It is like a burned rope: it cannot tie you up because it is empty of essence.[2] The thought-like occurrence is actually the shining radiance of emptiness. There is no difference between thought and emptiness. The Great Orgyen[3] said:

> Since the essence of thought is empty, know it as dharmakaya.

If you were to meditate it would be conceptual, so be without anything on which to meditate. Rest in regular thought. If you meddle with it then it is the deluded chain of ordinary thought, so don't contrive in any way. When you wander from resting in that immediacy it is real delusion, so there must be no wandering. Just that is enough: a nondistractedness without focus on any reference point. Dzogchen Guru Zhiwa said:

ཡེངས་པ་དགོས་ཏེ་དེ་གཅིག་པུས་ཆོག་དམིགས་པ་གང་ལ་ཡང་མ་གཏད་ཅིང་མ་ཡེངས་པ་གཅིག་གོ། རྫོགས་ཆེན་གུ་རུ་ཞི་བ་ལས། སྒོམ་མ་སྒོམ་དང་འབྲལ་མ་སྒོམ། མི་སྒོམ་དོན་དང་མི་འབྲལ་བ། ཞེས་པ་གང་ཤར་སྒོམ་ཡིན་པས་ན་བློས་བཅོས་པའི་སྒོམ་རྒྱུ་མེད་པས་སྒོམ་མ་སྒོམ། ཡེ་ནས་དོན་མེད་འཆལ་བ་མིན་པས་རང་ཐོག་ཏུ་འཇོག་པ་དེ་དང་འབྲལ་མ་སྒོམ། མི་སྒོམ་དོན་དེ་ལྟ་བུ་དང་རྒྱུན་དུ་མི་འབྲལ་བར་གྱིས་ཞེས་པའི་དོན་ནོ། འདི་ལ་དབང་པོ་ཁྱད་པར་གྱིས་ཞག་བདུན་ནམ་བཅུ་བཞིའམ་ཟླ་བ་གཅིག་ལས་ཆེད་འཛིན་གྱིས་མ་ཡེངས་པ་དེ་ལ་བརྩོན་མི་དགོས་པར་གང་ཤར་རྩོལ་མེད་དུ་འཇོག་ཐུབ་པ་གཅིག་འོང་། འདི་ལ་རྫོགས་ཆེན་པ་ཡི་གྲོལ་གླིང་ཡངས་ཀྱི་དགོངས་པ་ཟེར། ཕྱག་ཆེན་པ་རང་གསལ་གྱི་དྲན་པ་ཟེར་འདུ་གདའ། དེའི་རྒྱུན་མ་ཆད་པར་བསྐྱངས་པས་རྣམ་པ་ཐ་མལ་གྱི་ཤེས་པ་འཇིག་རྟེན་པའི་རྣམ་རྟོག་རང་ག་དང་ཁྱད་པར་སྤུ་ཙམ་ཡང་མེད་ལ། ངོ་བོ་དེར་འཛིན་མེད་པའི་ས་ལེ་ཧྲིག་གེ་བ་མཉམ་བཞག་ཡུལ་ཕུད། རྗེས་ཐོབ་རྐང་སྟོང་། བག་ཆགས་གཡའ་དག་པའི་ཤེས་པ་ངོས་བཟུང་དང་བྲལ་ཀྱང་རྣམ་རྟོག་ལྟར་སྣང་བ་ཅིག་འོང་། དེ་ཆོས་སྐུ་དངོས་ཡིན། རྫོགས་ཆེན་སེམས་ཕྱོགས་པས། རྣམ་རྟོག་མི་མངའ་ཅིར་ཡང་སལ་ལེར་མཁྱེན་བྱ་བའང་འདི་ལ་ཟེར་ཏེ། གྲུབ་ཆེན་མི་ཏྲ་ཛོ་ཀིས། ཅིར་སྣང་དྲང་པོར་བཞག་ན་བྱ་བྲལ་ལྷུན་གྱིས་གྲུབ། ཅེས་གསུངས། དེ་ལྟར་འཛིན་པའི་རྣམ་རྟོག་རང་གིས་རང་གྲོལ་བ་ན། ཕྱི་གཟུང་བའི་ཡུལ་གཟུགས་སྒྲ་ལ་སོགས་པའང་རང་གྲོལ་དུ་ཤུགས་ཀྱིས་འགྲོ་སྟེ་མིག་གི་ཡུལ་དུ་གཟུགས་བཟང་ངན། རྣ་བར་སྒྲ་སྙན་མི་སྙན་དེ་བཞིན་དུ་དྲི་རོ་རེག་བྱ་རྣམས་ཀྱི་བཟང་ངན་དང་། སེམས་བདེ་སྡུག་ཆགས་སྡང་། དགྲ་གཉེན་ས་ཆུ་མེ་རླུང་ལ་སོགས་པ་མདོར་ན་གང་ཤར་གང་སྣང་དེ་ག་ལ་བཟོ་བཅོས་མེད་པར་འཇོག་པ་ཡིན་ཏེ། རྫོགས་ཆེན་ལས། སྒོ་ལྔའི་རྣམ་ཤེས་གསལ་བ་ལ། ཡིད་ཀྱི་ཞེན་རྟོག་མ་ཞུགས་ན། རྒྱལ་བའི་

> Not experiencing meditation, not experiencing departure from it:
> Do not depart from the meaning of no meditation.

That is to say, since whatever arises is meditation, there is no mind-made thing to meditate on, hence "not experiencing meditation." Since there was never any way to deviate into meaninglessness, resting in that immediacy is "not experiencing departure." "Do not depart" ever from that kind of "meaning of no meditation."

Persons of special capability need not pursue this undistractedness for more than seven or fourteen days or one month. Without striving, there will come an ability to rest without effort in whatever arises. In the Great Completion this is called "the perspective of eternally free open space." It is like "the minding of innate clarity" in the Great Seal. When you cultivate its continuity without interruption, there won't be a speck of difference between the manifestation of ordinary mind and the regular thoughts of a worldly person. However, the clarity and transparency of not grasping at an essence there relieves the sitting meditation of an object, and the postmeditation will be empty of basis. Mind polished of habitual conditioning, even without recognition, still experiences thought-like occurrence. That is the actual dharmakaya. In the Mind Class teachings of the Great Completion, the phrase "without having thoughts, anything is clearly knowable" refers to this. The accomplished Mitrayogin[4] said:

> When one rests directly in whatever occurs, it is spontaneous presence free of activity.

In this way, if thoughts are naturally freed by themselves, then the objective, external objects, such as form, sound, and so on, will also be liberated as a natural consequence of this innate freedom. Thus, the visual objects of good and bad forms, the pleasant and unpleasant sounds in the ears, and similarly good and bad smells, tastes, objects of touch, mental attachment to happiness and aversion to suffering, enemies, friends, earth, water, fire, wind, and so on—in short, whatever arises, whatever appears—the point is to rest without fabrication in that very thing. As is said in the Great Completion:

> When the clinging thoughts of mind do not enter
> The clarity of the five sense consciousnesses—
> That is exactly the perspective of the victorious ones.

དགོངས་པ་དེ་ཀ་རང་། ཞེས་དང་། ཞི་བྱེད་པས། དོན་གོ་རྟོག་པའི་མཚང་རིག་ན། རྣམ་རྟོག་ཤར་ཚེ་གནས་པ་ཆེ། ཉོན་མོངས་རགས་ཚེ་ཡེ་ཤེས་གསལ། ཅེས་བཞེད་དོ། དེ་བས་ན་རྫོགས་པ་ཆེན་པོའི་དགོངས་པ་ནི། གང་ཤར་དེ་སྤྱོངས་ཡང་མི་སྤྱོང་། དེའི་རྗེས་སུ་ཡང་མི་འབྲང་། དེ་ཀ་ལ་བཅས་བཅོས་མི་བྱེད་པར་འཇོག་པ་འདི་ཀ་ཡིན་ནོ། དེ་ཡིན་པས་དེ་ལ་སྤང་བྱ་མེད། གཉེན་པོ་མེད། དགག་སྒྲུབ་བླང་དོར་ལ་སོགས་པ་བློ་བྱས་ཀྱི་ཆོས་གང་ཡང་མེད་པས་ན། བློ་འདས་ཆོས་སྐུ་དེ་བཞིན་ཉིད། ཅེས་པའང་དེ་ཡིན། དེ་དག་ནི་དབང་པོ་རབ་ཀྱི་དབང་དུ་བྱས་པ་ཡིན་པས། རབ་ཀྱི་རབ་འབྲིང་ཐ་མ་གསུམ་ལ་སོ་སོའི་བློ་ནུས་དང་སྦྱར་ཏེ་འཁྲིད་ཤེས་པར་བྱའོ། དབང་པོ་འབྲིང་གསུམ་ནི་ཞི་ལྷག་ཟུང་འབྲེལ་གྱི་སྒོ་ནས་འཁྲིད་པར་བྱ་སྟེ། དེ་ཡང་རྒྱལ་བ་ཡང་དགོན་པས། ཡི་བསྒོམ་ལ་བློ་ཡིས་མ་བསྒོམ་མཛོད། རང་བབས་ལ་བཟོ་ཡིས་མ་བཅོས་མཛོད། བློ་རྟོག་ལ་སྐྱོན་དུ་མ་ལྟ་བར། མི་རྟོག་པ་ཆེད་དུ་མ་སྒོམ་པར། སེམས་རང་ལུགས་སུ་ཞོག་ལ་རྒྱངས་སོ་ཚུག སྒོམ་ཞི་གནས་ཀྱི་མཐིལ་དུ་ཐེབས་པ་གཅིག་འོང་གི། ཞེས་དེ་ཀ་ལྟར་གོམས་འདྲིས་བྱེད་པ་ལ། གཟུགས་བསྒྲིངས་པས་འགྱུ་བ་ཇེ་ཉུང་ལ་སོང་། སེམས་ཀྱི་གནས་པ་ཇེ་བརྟན་ལ་འགྲོ། འདི་ལ་དྲན་པ་སླེབ་ན་ཞི་ལྷག་ཟུང་འབྲེལ་ཡིན། དེའི་རྒྱུན་བསྐྱངས་ནས་སྒོམ་པས་རྣམ་རྟོག་ཕྲ་རག་ཀུན། འགགས་ཏེ་ཏིང་ངེ་འཛིན་གྱི་ངོ་བོ་གང་དུའང་མ་གྲུབ་པའི་སྟོང་པ། གསལ་ལ་རྟོག་པ་མེད་པ་ལུས་སེམས་ཡོད་དུ་མི་ཚོར་ལ། ཏིང་ངེ་འཛིན་དེ་དང་འབྲལ་མི་ཕོད་པའི་བདེ་ཉམས་ཅན་གཅིག་འཆར། དེ་སྨུ་མཐུད་ནས་བསྒོམ་པས་སྤྱན་ལྔ་དང་། མངོན་ཤེས་ཀྱི་ཡོན་ཏན་ཀྱང་འབྱུང་སྟེ་བསམ་གཏན་ཟེར། ཞི་གནས་འཐུག་པོ་དེ་བསྒོམ་ནས་བསམ་གཏན་བཞི་དང་སྐྱེ་མཆེད་མུ་བཞིའི་ཏིང་ངེ་འཛིན་རྩེ་གཅིག་པ་སྟེ། མཐར་གྱིས་གནས་པའི་སྙོམས་པར་འཇུག་པ་དགུ་ཟེར། དགུ་པོ་འདི་མུ་སྟེགས་པ་ལའང་ཡོད་པས་ཕྱི་ནང་

And from the standpoint of Pacification:[5]

> Knowing how to unlock the secret of thought:
> When thought arises it is the great stillness;
> When blatant afflictive emotion, it is illuminating wisdom.

Therefore, the perspective of the Great Completion is not to reject whatever arises, but also not to follow after it. Resting in that itself without meddling is exactly it. That being so, there is no thing to reject, no remedy, no dos and don'ts, no keeping and discarding, etc. Since there are no mind-made phenomena whatsoever, "nonconceptual dharmakaya suchness" is also this.

This is according to the level of best capability. You should know how to guide those of the three subdivisions of the best—best, average, and lesser—by application to their individual mental abilities.

## Average Capability

People of the three kinds of average capability should be guided by means of the combination of calm abiding and superior insight. Gyalwa Yangönpa[6] said:

> In pristine meditation, do not meditate with the intellect.
> Do not contrive an undisturbed state through fabrication.
> Do not regard thoughts as faults.
> Do not meditate for the sake of nonthought.
> Rest in mind's own way, and keep watch from a distance.
> Meditate, and you will arrive at the core of calm abiding.

By becoming adept at just that with persistence, the movement of mind will decrease and mental stillness will become more stable. When mindfulness is applied to this, it is the combination of calm abiding and superior insight. Maintaining that continuity and meditating, all subtle and blatant thoughts are stopped. The essence of that absorption is empty of any existence whatsoever. In that clarity without thought there is no sensation of having a body and mind. There arises an experience of bliss in which you can scarcely bear to be parted from that absorption. If that is prolonged in meditation, the qualities such as "five eyes"[7] and clairvoyance[8] will occur. This

ཐུན་མོང་གི་ལམ་ཡིན་ཀྱང་། རྣམ་རྟོག་འཕྲོ་མང་ནས་ཁ་བྲི་མ་ཐུབ་པ་དེ་ལ་ཐོག་མར་ཞི་གནས་བཙལ་དགོས་པ་ཡིན། དེ་ལ་ཡང་ལྷག་མཐོང་མེད་ན་ས་ལམ་མི་བགྲོད་པས་སེམས་ཀྱི་གནས་ཆ་ཙམ་རྙེད་ནས་རྣམ་རྟོག་འདི་མ་འཕྲོས་ན་དགའ་བ་ལ་སྙམ་པའི་དུས་དེར་རྣམ་རྟོག་དེ་རང་ངོ་ཤེས་ཙམ་བྱས་ལ་ཁོ་རང་གི་ངོ་ལ་བལྟས་པས་ཡལ་ཏེ་གནས་པ་དང་གཅིག་ཏུ་སོང་བ་ནི་ཞི་ལྷག་ཟུང་འཇུག་གམ་ཟུང་འབྲེལ་བྱ་བ་ཡིན། དྭགས་པོ་བཀའ་བརྒྱུད་པས་གནས་འགྱུའི་བར་ལག་འགྲིལ་བ་ཟེར། ངོ་བོ་བློས་བྱས་པའི་བསྒོམ་ཡིན། འདི་ལ་ངོ་ཤེས་ཀྱི་དྲན་པ་དང་མ་བྲལ་བར་དགོས་པས་བཀའ་བརྒྱུད་པས་སྟོང་ཉིད་གཟུང་དྲན་ཟེར། འདི་ཀ་རྒྱུན་བསྐྱངས་ནས་བསྒོམ་པས་གཟུང་དྲན་དེ་རང་གསལ་གྱི་དྲན་པར་འགྲོ། མ་ཡེངས་པ་རང་བྱས་ན་འདི་ཡང་ཁ་གཟེ་མོ་གཅིག་ཡིན་ཏེ། ཟླ་བ་གཅིག་ཙམ་ནས་ཉིན་སྣང་འདྲེས་ཐུབ། རྒྱལ་བ་རྒོད་ཚང་པས། སྣང་བ་ཐམས་ཅད་སྟོང་པར་མི་བསྒོམ། མི་སྟོང་པར་ཡང་མི་བསྒོམ་གང་ཤར་དེ་ལ་དྲན་པས་བཟུང་ན་ཟླ་བ་གཅིག་རང་གིས་ཆོག་སྟེ། སྤྲོས་བྲལ་དང་པོའི་རང་གནས་འོང་། ཞེས་གསུངས་པར། ཧྲིལ་གྱིས་དྲིལ་ན། ཤུར་གྱི་ཞི་གནས་ཀྱི་ཏིང་ངེ་འཛིན་དེ་རང་ངོ་ཤེས་པས་ཞི་ལྷག་ཟུང་འབྲེལ་ལ། ཕྱག་རྒྱ་ཆེན་པོ་རྫོགས་པ་ཆེན་པོ་ཞེས་ཟེར་ཏེ། ཡང་དགོན་པས། བློ་རྟོག་པ་འགྱུ་བ་གནས་ལུགས་ཀྱི་སྒོ། རང་ངོ་ཤེས་པ་ཉམས་ལེན་གྱི་གནད། ཅེས་གསུངས་པ་ལ་འདུའོ། འདི་ལ་འཁྲིད་གི་འཁྲིད་དང་ཐ་མ་གཉིས་ཀྱིས་རྣམ་རྟོག་རང་ག་མ་དེ་སྒོམ་ཡིན་པར་ཡིད་ལ་མི་བྱེད་ན། རྣམ་རྟོག་གང་ཤར་དེ་ལ་བལྟས་པས་ཐམས་ཅད་སྟོང་པར་ཡལ། ཡལ་བ་དེའི་ངང་ནས་གཅིག་རྟིང་ལ་གཅིག་འཆར། དེ་ལ་ཡང་བལྟས་པས་ཤུར་ལྷུར་ཡལ་དེ་ཁའི་རྒྱུད་སྐྱོང་བ་ཡིན་ཏེ། མགུར་ལས། སེམས་ངོས་བཟུང་མེད་པ་སྟོང་པའི་དབྱིངས། སྣ་ཚོགས་སུ་འཆར་བ་རིག་པའི་སྒོམ། བློ་བྲལ་གྱི་གསལ་སྟོང་རྗེན་པ་འདིའི། ངང་ལ་བཞག་བཞིན་དབྱིངས་ལ་ལྟོས་དང་།

is called "meditative concentration." Meditating in that deep calm abiding, four concentrations[9] and single-pointed absorption in four spheres of perception[10] will occur. Ultimately, what are called "the nine equilibriums of abiding"[11] will occur. These nine are also possessed by heretics[12] and so it is the common path of both Buddhists and non-Buddhists.

But if there are too many active thoughts and you cannot reduce them, you should first pursue calm abiding. However, without superior insight[13] there can be no progress in the stages and paths. Therefore, when you practice with just the aspect of mental abiding, and you feel pleased that thought is not emanating, just recognize *that* thought and look at its very own essence. Then it will dissipate. It has become one with the abiding. This, then, is called the unity or combination of calm abiding and superior insight. The Dagpo Kagyus call this "collapsing the boundary between stillness and movement." Essentially, it is a mind-made meditation. You need to have mindful recognition constantly, and so the Kagyus call it "mindful holding of emptiness." Maintaining the continuity of this itself in meditation, that mindful holding will become the mindfulness of innate clarity. Just being undistracted in that is very important. In just one month you will be able to integrate it with daytime appearances. Gyalwa Götsangpa[14] said:

> Do not meditate on the emptiness of all appearances,
> Nor meditate on their non-emptiness.
> If you are mindful and hold whatever arises,
> Then just one month is sufficient.
> The innate abiding in the first stage of freedom from
> embellishment[15] will come.

To wrap it up: the self-recognition of the initial absorption of calm abiding is the combination of calm abiding and superior insight. That is the Great Seal and the Great Completion. It is summarized in this quotation from Yangon:

> The movement of conceptual thought is the door to true nature.
> Self-recognition of it is the crucial point of practice.

### *The Average and Lesser Subdivisions of the Average*

The average and lesser of the average type may not be able to accept that the regular thought process *is* the meditation, so you should look at what-

བསྒོམ་ལྷག་མཐོང་གི་མཐིལ་དུ་ཕེབས་པ་གཅིག་འོང་གི། ཞེས་གསུངས་པ་བཞིན་ཉམས་སུ་ལེན། འདི་ལ་མི་ཏྲ་ཛོ་ཀིས། གང་ཤར་ངོ་ཡིས་བཟུང་བ་རིག་པ་རང་སར་གྲོལ། ཞེས་པས། ལས་སླ་ལ་ཆུན་ཆེ་བ་གཅིག་ཡིན་ནོ། རབ་འབྲིང་གསུམ་ཀའི་ཐུན་མོང་དུ་སྒོམ་ལུགས་ནི། མགུར་ལས། མ་ཡེངས་དྲན་པ་སོ་མ་ཤོར། མ་བསྒོམ་པའི་གནས་ལུགས་བཟོ་མ་བྱས། བསམ་མེད་ཀྱི་རིག་པ་སྨྲ་མ་འདོད། རྟག་ཆད་ཀྱི་མ་བསླད་ཡུན་དུ་སྐྱོངས་དང་། བསྒོམ་ཞི་ལྷག་ཟུང་དུ་ཆུད་པ་གཅིག་འོང་གི། ཞེས་གསུངས་པ་གོ་སླ་ཡང་། དྲན་པ་མ་ཡེངས་པས་གང་ཤར་ལ་བཟོ་བཅོས་མི་བྱེད། ཤར་ཡང་ཡོད་པར་མི་བལྟ། ཡལ་ཡང་མེད་པར་མི་འཛིན། རྣམ་རྟོག་གི་སྣ་མི་བསྐྱིལ་བར་འགྲོ་བཙུག་ནས་ངོ་ཤེས་ཙམ་བྱེད་པའོ། རྫོགས་ཆེན་སེམས་སྡེ་ལས། གདོད་ནས་དག་པ་དབྱིངས་ཀྱི་དང་ཉིད་ནས། རིག་པ་ཐད་སྐྱེས་སྐད་ཅིག་དྲན་པ་དེ། རྒྱ་མཚོའི་གཏིང་ནས་ནོར་བུ་རྙེད་པ་འདྲ། སུས་ཀྱང་མ་བཅོས་མ་བྱས་ཆོས་ཀྱི་སྐུ། ཞེས་གསུངས་པ་ལྟར་ངོ་སྤྲོད་དོ། དབང་པོ་ཐ་མ་གསུམ་ནི། ཐལ་ཆེར་ལྷག་མཐོང་ལ་ཡིད་མི་ཆེས། ཞི་གནས་གཤའ་མ་ཡང་སྐྱེ་མི་ཐུབ་སྟེ། རེས་བྲིངས། རེས་རྒོད་ནས་སྒོམ་མི་འཆར་བས། སྔོན་འགྲོ་མཐར་ཕྱིན་རྫོགས་པ་དང་། སྟན་བདེ་བར་རྐང་པ་སྐྱིལ་ཀྲུང་། ལག་པ་མཉམ་བཞག་ལྟེ་ཡར་རྐན་ལ་སྦྱར། མིག་སྣ་རྩེར་ཕབ་པ་སོགས་ཆོས་བདུན་ཚང་བར་བྱས་ཤིང་། རླུང་རོ་དགུ་ཕྱུགས་སུ་ཕྱུད་ལ། སྤྱི་བོའམ་སྙིང་ཁར་བླ་མ་བསྒོམ་ཞིང་གསོལ་བ་བཏབ། ལུས་སེམས་ལྷོད་ཀྱིས་སློད་པའི་ངང་ནས་རྣམ་རྟོག་གང་ཤར་དེ་ཀ་ལ་བལྟས་ནས་དེ་རང་གི་ཐོག་ཏུ་ལྷོད་ཀྱིས་སློད། ཡང་ཤར་ན་དེའི་ཐོག་ཏུ་སྔར་ལྟར་སློད། ཡལ་ནས་སྟོང་པར་སོང་བ་དེའི་དགའ་བྲོད་མི་བྱ། རྣམ་རྟོག་མང་པོར་སོང་བ་ལ་སྐྱོན་དུ་མི་བལྟ། སྒོམ་ཡོང་དུ་རེ་བ་དང་མ་བྱུང་བའི་དོགས་པ་གཉིས་ཀ་མི་བྱ། གང་ཤར་གྱི་སྟེང་དུ་ལྷོད་དེ་འཇོག། ལྷོད་ཆེན་རྣམ་རྟོག་མེད་པའི་མི་རྟོག་པ་འདྲ་མོ་འགྱུ་

ever thoughts arise and they will all disappear in emptiness. Within that disappearance, while one thought subsides another arises. Again watching that, it disappears as before. It is maintaining the continuity of just that, as in the song:

> Mind, unidentifiable, is the expanse of emptiness.
> The variety that arises is the door of awareness.
> Free of concept, stark, empty, clear.
> Resting within this, regard the expanse.
> You will arrive at the pith of superior insight meditation.

Practice accordingly. In this regard Mitrayogin also said,

> By identifying whatever arises,
> Awareness is liberated in its own ground.

This is simple but of great impact.

### *All Three Subdivisions of Average*

The meditation held in common for the best, average, and lesser of the average capability is as taught in this song:

> No distraction: sharp mindfulness is not lost.
> No meditation: true nature is not fabricated.
> No desire to speak of unthinkable awareness.
> Continuing, uncorrupted by permanence or nihilism.
> Meditating, the union of calm abiding and superior insight will come.

This is easily understood. With undistracted mindfulness, do not meddle with whatever arises. Although it arises, do not regard it as existent. Although it disappears, do not grasp it as nonexistent. Without suppressing them, just let the thoughts go, sustaining mere recognition. As is stated in the Mind Class of Great Completion:

> From within the very expanse of original purity,
> Mindful each moment of the immanent arising of awareness,

དྲན་གང་ཡང་མེད་པ་གཅིག་འོང་བས། དེ་དྲན་པས་གྲིམ་གྱིས་སྒྲིམ་ཏེ་ངོ་ཤེས་པ་མ་བྱས་ན་རང་གིས་མི་ཚོར་བར་རྟོག་པ་འོག་འགྲུ་ཕུབ་མའི་འོག་གི་ཆུ་དོང་ལྟ་བུ་གཅིག་ཡོད། དེས་འཕྲུལ་དུ་མི་གནོད་པ་ལྟར་ལ་ཕུགས་སུ་ཁོ་རྒྱལ་ནས་སྒོམ་ཡོངས་སུ་མི་སྟེར་བས་སྒྲིམ་དགོས། རྟོག་པ་ཁ་འགྲུ་ནི་ངོས་ཟིན་པའི་འགྲུ་དྲན་ཚེ་ཡིན་པས་དེ་ཐོག་ཏུ་སློད་ནས་འཇོག ཇི་ཞིག་ནས་རྣམ་རྟོག་མང་དུ་སོང་ནས་རང་ཚིག་པ་ཟ། ངལ་སྒོམ་མི་ཡོང་བར་འདུག་སྙམ་པ་འོང་སྟེ་སྐྱོན་མེད། ཉམས་དང་པོ་རི་གཟར་གྱི་ཆུ་ལྟ་བུ་བྱ་བ་དེ་བཀའ་བརྒྱུད་པས་རྩེ་གཅིག་རྟོག་པའི་ཟླ་ལ་གཡེང་ཟེར་ཏེ་རྩེ་གཅིག་ཆུང་ངུའི་སྐབས་ཡིན། དེ་ཀ་ལ་སྲན་བསྐྱེད་དེ་སྒོམ་པས། སྐབས་རེ་སྡོད། སྐབས་རེ་འཕྲོ་བ་ཆུ་ནང་གི་བྱེའུ་ཆུལ་རེས་འཛུལ་རེས་འཐོན། སྐབས་རེ་རྡོ་སྟེང་དུ་བག་རེ་སྡོད་པ་དང་འདྲ། ཉམས་གཉིས་པའི་སྐྱེ་ལུགས་ཡིན། ཡང་མུ་མཐུད་དེ་སྒོམ་ན་རེ་ཞིག་ནས་སྐབས་རེ་འཕྲོ་ཡང་། ཤས་ཆེར་གནས་པ་འདྲ་བ་གཅིག་འོང་། དཔེ་མི་རྒན་དང་འདྲ་སྟེ་སྡོད་པ་ཤས་ཆེ། ཉམས་གསུམ་པའི་སྐྱེ་ལུགས་ཡིན། ཡང་རྒྱུན་མཐུད་པས་རེ་ཞིག་ན་སྦུབ་མང་གི་སྲུར་བའི་ཆུ་ལྟར་འཕྲོ་བ་མི་མངོན་པའོ། འདི་དུས་ཀྱང་དྲན་པ་ཅུང་ཟད་སྒྲིམ་དགོས། ཉམས་བཞི་པའི་སྐྱེ་ལུགས་ཡིན། དེ་རྒྱུན་མཐུད་པས་ཇི་ཞིག་ན་སེམས་གང་དུ་མི་འཕྲོ་བར་ཉིན་མཚན་ཀུན་ཏུ་གནས་པས་སྒོམ་དང་གོས་ཀྱི་སྲིད་པ་ཡང་མི་འབྱུང་ཞིང་། གཡོ་འགུལ་མེད་པ་ཞག་དང་ཟླ་བ་སྐྱོལ་བར་གནས་པས་དཔེ་རི་བོ་ལྟ་བུ་སྟེ། འདི་ཉེས་ན་ཁ་ཐལ་ན་ཉན་ཐོས་འགོག་པར་འགྲོ། ལེགས་ན་ལུས་ཤིན་སྦྱངས་ཐོབ་ནས་ཞི་གནས་ཕུལ་དུ་ཕྱིན་པ་ཡིན། ཉམས་ལྔ་པའི་སྐྱེ་ལུགས་ཡིན། འདི་དག་ཀྱང་གཙོ་ཆེ་བའི་དབང་དུ་བྱས་ཀྱི། གང་ཟག་སོ་སོའི་རྩ་ཁམས་དང་དབང་པོའི་རིམ་པ་ལ་གཅིག་ཏུ་མ་ངེས་པ་ཡང་སྲིད་དོ། དེ་ཚེ་དབང་པོ་ཐ་མའི་རབ་ལ་རིམ་པས་ཡོང་མོད་ཀྱིས་འབྲིང་ཐ་གཉིས་ལ་གནས་པ་སྐྱེ་དཀའ་བས། ལུས་གནད་སྔར་ལྟར་ལ། མདུན་

> It is like finding a gem in the ocean's depths.
> Nobody has contrived or tampered with dharmakaya.

In this way it is revealed.

## Three Kinds of Lesser Capability

### *Calm Abiding*

The three types of individuals of lesser capability for the most part do not believe in superior insight[16] and are not able to generate calm abiding alone. They alternate between torpor and agitation, and meditation does not arise. Therefore, you should complete the entire preliminary practice. Then, sit in cross-legged posture on a comfortable seat with hands in meditation position, tongue touching the palate, eyes falling in front of the nose, and so on—all seven positions of meditation. Do the nine-breath exercise to clear away stale breath, and pray while meditating on the guru above your head or in your heart. Within a state of relaxation of body and mind, look right at whatever thought arises and relax directly in that itself. When another arises, relax directly into it as before. Do not rejoice when thought has vanished into emptiness, and do not see it as problematic when it multiplies. Do not entertain either hope for meditation to go well or fear that it will not occur well. Relax right into whatever arises. If you are too relaxed, there comes an experience of no conscious thought process whatsoever, a lack of thought similar to nonthought.[17] Then you should tighten up your attention with mindfulness, because without recognition you will not feel the discursive undercurrent, which is like trenches of water underneath husks of grain. It will not cause any harm immediately, but eventually it will win out and withhold genuine meditation, so close attentiveness is necessary.

Obvious discursiveness is the time for the identification of the conscious thought process, so stay relaxed directly on that. At some point, thoughts might proliferate and you will get irritated at yourself. You think, "meditation is just not happening for me." No problem. That is the first meditative experience, "like a waterfall off a steep cliff." The Kagyus call it "undivided attention that is distracted by the waves of thought." It is the occasion of the lesser undivided attention.[18] If you bear with that and continue meditating, sometimes it will stay, sometimes be active. It's like a little bird in the water, sometimes slipping in and out of the water, sometimes resting for a

ཏུ་སྨིན་མཚམས་ཀྱི་ཐད་འདོམས་གང་ཙམ་གྱི་སར་ཤིང་བུ་གཅིག་བཙུགས་ནས། དེ་ལ་
ཡིད་དམིགས་རླུང་གསུམ་དྲིལ་ལ་གཏད་དེ། སེམས་མི་འཕྲོ་བའི་རྟེན་ཙམ་དུ་བྱས་ལ།
སྒྲིམ་ཆེན་སུན་སྐྱེན། ལྷོད་ཆེན་སྒོམ་འཚེར་བས་རན་པར་ཐུན་ཆུང་ལ་གྲངས་མང་བར་
བྱ། དེ་ནས་རིམ་པར་ཐུན་ཆེ་ལ་གྲངས་ཉུང་དུ་བཏང་། སེམས་གནས་པར་སོང་ན་ཤིང་བུ་
དེའི་རྩེ་མོར་ཨ་དཀར་པོ་གཅིག་བསམ་ལ་ཕྱུར་ལྷུར་བསྒོམ། དེ་ནས་ཐིག་ལེ་དཀར་པོ་
དང་སེར་པོ་ལ་སོགས་རིམ་པས་སྦྱོ་ཞིང་དམིགས་རྟེན་རེ་ལ་ཞག་གཅིག་གམ་གསུམ་
ལ་སོགས་པར་མ་སུན་བར་བྱས་ལ་ཅི་རིགས་སུ་བསྒོམ། ཡང་ཤིང་བུའི་ཤུལ་དུ་རྡེའུ་
གཅིག་བཞག་ལ་ཕྱུར་སྤུར་རིམ་པས་བསྒོམ། དེ་ནས་རང་ལུས་ཀྱི་གནས་གསུམ་དང་།
ནང་གི་མགྲིན་པ་སྙིང་ཁ་རྣམས་སུ་ཡིག་འབྲུ་དང་ཐིག་ལེ་སོགས་གང་རིགས་ལ་
དམིགས་རྟེན་བཅས་ཏེ་བསྒོམས་པས་རིམ་གྱིས་གནས་པ་བརྟན་པར་འགྱུར་རོ། དེ་ཡང་
ངང་ཐུང་མི་བྱ་བར་རིམ་གྱིས་གོམས་བཙུག་ཅིང་མི་སུན་པ་བྱ་བ་གལ་ཆེའོ། ཞི་གནས་
ཀྱི་སྐབས་འདིར་ཐུག་བཅེར་དུ་མ་སོང་བར་ཕྱར་གྱི་འཛོག་ལུགས་ལ་མ་ཡེངས་པ་རལ་
སྐོར་མཁན་གཡུལ་ཀུ་ཞུགས་པ་ལྟ་བུ་གསུངས། དེ་ཡང་རལ་བསྐོར་མཁན་སྐད་ཅིག་
ཀྱང་མ་ཡེངས་ན་མདའ་མཁན་གྱི་མདའ་འཕང་ཚད་རལ་གྲིས་བླངས་ཏེ་ཕོལ་མི་ཐོག་པ་
ལ། བུ་མེད་མཛེས་མའི་སྤྱོད་ལམ་ལ་མིག་སྐད་ཅིག་ཡེངས་པས་ཕོ་ལ་མདའ་ཐོག་ཏེ་
འཆི་ཁ། མདའ་ཡིས་མ་ལན་ཡེངས་པས་ལན། ཕྱིན་ཆད་རལ་བསྐོར་མཁན་པོ་ཀུན།
སྐད་ཅིག་ཙམ་ཡང་མ་ཡེངས་ཅིག་ཡེངས་ནང་བཞིན་སྟོག་དང་བྲལ། ཟེར་ནས་ཤིའོ།
དཔེ་དེ་བཞིན་དུ་མ་ཡེངས་པ་གལ་ཆེའོ། དེ་ནི་ལྷག་མཐོང་སྔོན་ཏེ། ལྷག་མཐོང་ནི་
ཤེས་རབ་ཀྱི་ཕ་རོལ་ཏུ་ཕྱིན་པ་ཞེས་བྱ་བ་ཡིན་ཏེ། འདི་མེད་ན་ས་ལམ་མི་བགྲོད་པས་
ཕར་ཕྱིན་གཞན་རྣམས་མིག་མེད་པ་དང་འདྲ་བར་བཤད་ཅིང་། རྗེ་སྒམ་པོ་པས། མཉམ་
བཞག་གཅིག་གིས་ཞག་བདུན་ཐུབ་པ་བྱུང་གསུངས་པ་ལ་རྗེ་མི་ལས་བསམ་གཏན་

bit on a rock. This is how the second meditative experience arises. If that is prolonged further in meditation, from time to time there will be occasional mental activity, but for the most part there is abiding. For example, it is like an old person who sits still most of the time. This is how the third meditative experience arises. When that is prolonged continually, at some point mental activity will not be in evidence, like water in the small rivulets of the underbrush. At that time, mindfulness needs to be somewhat tightened. This is how the fourth meditative experience arises. If the continuity of that is prolonged in that way, eventually the mind will be still day and night without budging. Thirst and the desire for clothes won't even arise. As you abide without any movement, days and months will pass. The example is that of a mountain. If this goes wrong and gets excessive, it becomes the absorption of a hearer.[19] If it goes well, after you attain the total refinement of body, it will be supreme calm abiding. This is how the fifth meditative experience arises.[20]

This description, however, is according to the majority. It is likely that the process varies according to the individual's energetic constitution and capability.

That process will certainly occur for the best level of the lesser type of capability, but for those of the average and lesser levels of the lesser, it is difficult for stillness to occur. Therefore, such individuals should assume the physical posture as described before, and then plant a stick at the level of the eyebrows about four cubits in front of you. Mingling the mind, the visualization, and the subtle wind, focus on the stick. In making just this support for deactivating the mind, if you are too tight you will become easily jaded, and if too loose the meditation will go astray. So practice with moderation, doing many short sessions. Then gradually change to fewer, longer sessions. Once the mind begins to dwell over there, imagine a white letter AH on the tip of the stick and meditate as before. Then exchange the AH for a white sphere, a yellow sphere, and so on, meditating accordingly on each visualization support for one or three days or for as long as you do not become jaded. Again, replace the stick with a pebble and go through the meditation process as before. Then, using the visualization support of letters and spheres, meditate on the three places of your body, and in the inner forehead, throat, and heart in the appropriate way. Gradually, the abiding will become stabilized. It is important not to become impatient but to keep up the process until you establish familiarization without becoming jaded.

At this time of calm abiding do not push too hard—just remain

བཞིའི་ལྷའི་ཏིང་ངེ་འཛིན་དུ་ངོ་སྤྲོད་པ་ལྷ་བུའོ། ལྷག་མཐོང་ལ་གསུམ་སྟེ། ཆོས་རབ་ཏུ་རྣམ་པར་འབྱེད་པའི་ལྷག་མཐོང་ནི། མདོ་སྡེ་ཐམས་ཅད་ཀྱི་དགོངས་དོན་ཡིན་པའི་ལྷག་མཐོང་ཕྱིན་ཅི་མ་ལོག་པ་ཤེས་པ་ལ་ཟེར། སེམས་རང་བཞིན་གྱིས་རྣམ་པར་དག་པའི་གནས་ལུགས་ཇི་ལྟར་ཤེས་པའི་ལྷག་མཐོང་ནི། ད་ལྟ་ངོ་སྤྲོད་ཅིང་བསྒོམ་པ་ཡིན། འདི་གོམས་པས་གནས་ལུགས་ཕྱིན་ཅི་མ་ལོག་པ་མངོན་དུ་གྱུར་པའི་ལྷག་མཐོང་ནི། འབྲས་བུ་སངས་རྒྱས་ཐོབ་པའི་དུས་དེར་འབྱུང་ངོ་། ད་ཞི་གནས་ཀྱི་སྐབས་ལྟར་རྣམ་རྟོག་མཉམ་བཞག་ཏུ་བཤད་འདུག་ཀྱང་དེ་ངོ་ཤེས་ཙམ་ལ་བཞག་པས་ཆོག རྣམ་རྟོག་སྣ་ཚོགས་སུ་འགྱུ་ན་ཡང་དེ་ངོ་ཤེས་ཙམ་གྱི་ངང་དུ་འཛོག མདོར་ན་གང་ཤར་གང་བྱུང་ངོ་ཤེས་ཙམ་གྱི་ངང་དུ་འཛོག་པ་འདི་ཀ་ཡིན། བསྒོམ་ནས་བསྒོམ་རྒྱུ་ཅི་ཡང་མེད་དོ། སྤྱང་གཉེན་དུ་བལྟས་ནས་རྩོལ་སྒྲུབ་གང་བྱས་འཁོར་བའི་རྒྱུ་འབྲས་ལས་མ་འདས་སོ། དེ་ཡང་ཏིང་ངེ་འཛིན་གྱི་མི་མཐུན་པའི་ཕྱོགས་ནི་རྣམ་རྟོག་ཡིན་ལ་དེ་སྤྱངས་མི་དགོས་ལོ་བའི་སྟེང་དུ་ལོ་རང་བཞག་བཞག་པས་རང་དག་ལ་འགྲོ་བ་ཡིན། འཁྲུལ་སྣང་འཛིན་པ་བཟློག་སྤྱངས་མིན། མི་མཐུན་པ་ཉིད་གཉེན་པོར་རྫོགས། ཞེས་སོ། དབང་པོ་ཐ་མའི་ཐ་མས་དེ་ལྟར་བྱས་ཀྱང་སེམས་ལས་སུ་མ་རུང་ན་རྣམ་རྟོག་གང་སྐྱེས་དེ་ངོས་བཟུང་ནས་དེ་ཇི་ལྟར་འདུག་དང་། གར་འགྲོ་བལྟས་པས་རང་དག་ཏུ་འགྲོ་ཞིང་། དེའི་རྒྱུན་བསྐྱངས་པས་ཕྱིས་ཆེད་དུ་རྩད་མི་དགོས་པ་རྣམ་རྟོག་ལོས་ལོ་རང་གྲོལ་བར་བྱེད་དེ་རང་བྱུང་གི་ཡེ་ཤེས་ཞེས་བྱའོ། འགྱུ་བའི་རྩད་གདར་བཅད་ན་དེ་གཅིག་པོས་དྲན་རྟོག་དབྱིངས་སུ་ཡལ། ཞེས་པའི་དོན་ཏོ། སྤྱིར་ན་ཐ་མལ་གྱི་ཤེས་པ་ཞེས་བྱ་བ་རྣམ་རྟོག་གང་ཤར་ཀྱི་ངོ་བོ་ལ་བཟོ་བཅོས་མི་བྱེད་པ་འདི་ལས་མ་ཡེངས་ན་དེ་གཅིག་པུས་ཆོག་སྟེ། དབང་པོ་ཐ་མས་དེ་ལྟར་མི་འོང་བས་རྩོལ་བཅས་ཀྱི་མཉམ་བཞག་སྐྱོང་བ་ཡིན། རྣམ་རྟོག་གང་ཤར་ལ་བལྟས་ཀྱང་ཞི་མ་ནུས་པར་འཕྲོ་ཆེན། ལུས་གནད་བཤིག འཕྲོ་

undistracted in the initial way of placing the attention, like the proverbial swordsman at battle. There was a swordsman who was not distracted even for an instant and could catch all the arrows shot by an archer in his sword without being struck. But then for one instant the movement of a beautiful woman distracted his eye and an arrow struck him. At the moment of death he said:

> I am done in not by the arrow but by distraction.
> Henceforth, all you swordsmen,
> Do not be distracted for even an instant.
> In distraction life is lost.

Saying that, he died. As in this example, it is extremely important not to be distracted.

### *Superior Insight*

Now the presentation of superior insight: What is called superior insight is the perfection of transcendent intelligence. Without it there is no progress through the levels and paths, so it is explained that without it the other perfections are as if without eyes. For instance, when Lord Gampopa told Milarepa that he could remain for seven days in a single meditative equipoise, Milarepa pointed out the gods' absorption of the fourth concentration.[21]

Superior insight has three divisions. The superior insight of fully discerning phenomena is said to be the cognizance of unmistaken superior insight, the main perspective of all sutras and tantras. Superior insight that knows the manner of the naturally pure mind is the meditation on what has now been revealed. Once this is familiar, the superior insight of actualizing the unmistaken true nature arises in the fruition of attaining buddhahood.

Now, as with calm abiding, there is an explanation of meditative equipoise concerning thoughts. However, it is sufficient to rest in mere recognition. Even when various thoughts move, just rest within the state of mere recognition. In short, whatever arises and whatever occurs, rest within the state of merely recognizing it. That's it!

Meditating, there is absolutely no meditation subject. Looking for a remedy by rejecting something or pursuing any kind of accomplishment does not get beyond the cause and effect of cyclic existence. The antithesis of meditative absorption is discursive thought, but there is no need to reject it. Rather, let it rest in itself. Resting, it will become naturally pure. As is said:

མཁན་པོ་རང་འགྲོ་བཅུག་ནས་ཁོའི་ངང་དེ་ལ་བལྟས་པས་ཞི་མལ་གྱིས་འགྲོ། འགྲོ་བ་དང་གནས་པ་གཉིས་ཀ་སེམས་ཡིན་པས་རང་མལ་དུ་གཅིག་ཏུ་འགྱུར་ཏེ། སྒོམ་སྲུན་བསྐྱེད་པས་གཏིང་ཚུགས་པར་འགྱུར་རོ། དེ་ཡང་། ཇི་ལྟར་གཟིང་ལས་འཕུར་བའི་བྱ་རོག་ནི། བསྐོར་ཞིང་བསྐོར་ཞིང་སླར་ཡང་དེ་རུ་འབབ། ཅེས་པའི་དཔེས་སྟོན་ཏེ། རྒྱ་མཚོའི་ཟུར་ནས་བྱ་རོག་གི་རྐང་པར་ལྕུགས་ཐག་ཕྲ་མོས་བཏོང་དགོས་ལ། མཚོ་དཀྱིལ་དུ་སླེབ་ནས་ཡར་འཕུར་ན་ནམ་མཁའ་སྟོང་པ་ཕར་ཚུར་ནི་བར་སྣང་སྟོང་པ། འོག་ཏུ་ནི་རྒྱ་ལས་མ་འདས་པས་ཡར་མར་ཕྱོགས་མཚམས་གང་དུ་འཕུར་ཀྱང་འགྲོ་ས་དང་སླེབ་ས་མ་རྙེད་པས།སྔར་གྱི་ཤུལ་གཟིང་ཐོག་ཏུ་འབབ་པ་བཞིན་དུ། རྣམ་རྟོག་ཁོ་རང་འགྲོ་རུང་སྟོང་པ། མི་འགྲོ་རུང་སྟོང་པ། གནས་རུང་འགྱུ་རུང་སྟོང་པ་ལས་མ་འདས་པས། ཁོ་རང་གང་ཤར་དེ་ཁའི་ངང་དུ་བབས་པས་དབང་པོ་ཐ་མས་ཀྱང་རབ་ཀྱིས་སོར་འཛོག་ཏུ་འགྱུར་བས་ནན་ལྟར་གཟབ་པས་དཔྱད་ནས་འདི་ལ་བསླབ་ན་ལེགས་སོ། དེ་ལྟར་དབང་པོ་རབ་འབྲིང་ཐ་གསུམ་དགུ་ཕྲུགས་སུ་ཕྱེ་ནས་ཉམས་སུ་ལེན་ཚུལ་བསྟན་པ་སྣེ་རྫོགས་ཆེན་སྙན་བརྒྱུད་ལས། དབང་པོ་རབ་ལྟ་ཐོག་ནས་བསྒོམ་ནུས། འབྲིང་བསྒོམ་ཐོག་ནས་བསྒོམ་ནུས་ལ། ཐ་མ་སྤྱོད་ཐོག་ནས་སྒྲུབ་ནུས་པའོ། ཞེས་གསུངས་པའི་དགོངས་པའོ། དེ་ཡང་བསྒོམ་ལ་སྙིང་རུས་བསྐྱེད་དགོས་སྟེ། ཆོས་ཟབ་ཀྱང་མ་སྒོམ་ན་གདམས་ངག་ཟབ་མོ་དཔེ་ཆའི་ལོགས་ལ་ལུས་ཟེར་བ་དེ་ཡིན་མོད། ད་རེས་སྒོམ་རྒྱུད་ལ་ཐེབས་ཀྱང་། དུས་རྒྱུན་དུ་མ་བསྒོམ་ན་བློ་རྡེད་ཉམས་ལེན་རྡེད་ནས་འཆི་དུས་མི་ཕན་པས་གཟབ་དགོས། རྒྱལ་བ་རྒོད་ཚང་པས། ཕྱི་འཚམས་རི་ཁྲོད་དུ་སྡོད་ཚུགས་པ། ནང་འཚམས་སྤྱིལ་པོར་སྡོད་ཚུགས་པ། གསང་འཚམས་མལ་དུ་སྡོད་ཚུགས་པ། གཉིས་མེད་ལྟ་བའི་སྟེང་དུ་སྡོད་ཚུགས་པ། ཡེངས་མེད་བསྒོམ་པའི་སྟེང་དུ་སྡོད་ཚུགས་པ། ཆགས་མེད་སྤྱོད་པའི་སྟེང་དུ་སྡོད་ཚུགས་པ་དང་དྲུག་ཚང

> Do not avert or reject fixation on deluded appearances.
> The antithesis itself is complete in the remedy.

The lesser type of those of lesser capability might do that, but if your mind is not ready you should identify whatever thought arises and look at how it exists and where it goes. Then it will become pure naturally. By maintaining that continuity, afterward you will not need to purposefully pursue it—the thought will liberate itself. This is called innately occurring pristine wisdom. That is what is meant by the saying

> When mental movement is minutely investigated, thoughts will vanish into the expanse by that alone.

In general, what is called "ordinary mind" means not to meddle with whatever thought arises. If you are not distracted from this, it alone is sufficient. This will not work for those of lesser capability, so you should cultivate the sitting practice with effort. Though you look at whatever thought arises, without the ability to calm it down, there will be greater mental activity and the body posture will collapse. The one that is emanating thought—let that one emanate. Then look at its own state. It calms down in its own bed. Since mental activity and stillness are both the mind, they become one in their own bed. By engendering forbearance in meditation, it will be planted deeply. It is taught in this example:

> Like the crow that takes off from a ship:
> Circling, circling, again it lands on board.

The crow that was tied with fine wire to its feet when the ship was near the coast must be sent off after arriving in the middle of the ocean. Flying upward it finds that the sky is empty, and flying back down the space between is empty. Below there is nothing but water. Flying up and down and in all directions, it finds no place to go, no place to land. So it returns to the same ship and lands there.[22]

It is fine if a thought emanates—it is empty. It is fine if it does not emanate—it is empty. It is fine if it abides, fine if it moves—it does not get beyond empty. Whatever way it arises, it will fall back on itself. So even those of lesser capability who practice the technique of placement meditation of the best capability will do well with this training if they persist fastidiously and develop discernment.

དགོས་གསུངས། སྤྱིར་སྒོམ་ལ་ཡར་འཛུས་དང་ཚུར་འཛུས་གཉིས་ཡིན། སེམས་ལས་སུ་མ་རུང་བར་ལ་ཡར་འཛུས་བྱེད་དགོས་པས་དྲན་པ་དང་མི་བྲལ། དེ་ནས་རྣམ་རྟོག་ཁོ་རང་གིས་ཚུར་འཛུས་ནས་གང་ཤར་ཐམས་ཅད་སྒོམ་དུ་འགྲོ་བ་ཡིན། དེ་ཡང་ཐ་མལ་གྱི་ཤེས་པ་ཁོ་རང་ལ་འཛིན་པ་མེད་པའི་ངང་དུ་འགྲོ་བ་ཡིན་ནོ། བསྒོམ་ཆེན་པས་བསྒོམ་བཏང་ཀྱང་། བསྒོམ་གྱིས་བསྒོམ་ཆེན་པ་མི་གཏོང་བའི་དུས་ཟེར། དེ་འོང་པ་ལ་བར་མ་ཆད་དུ་བསྒོམ་དགོས། མ་བསྒོམ་ན་ད་ལྟ་ཉམས་མྱོང་ཕྲན་བུ་རེ་སྐྱེས་ཀྱང་ཡལ་འགྲོ་བས་བསྒོམ་འཇའ་ཚོན་མ་བྱ་བ་ཡིན། ལྷུགས་ཀྱུ་མ་བྱ་བ་དྲན་པས་ཟིན་དུས་ཡོད་ལ། མ་ཟིན་ན་མེད་པ་ཡིན་དེ་ལ་མ་ཡེངས་པ་བྱ་ར་བསྒྲིམ་དགོས། ཡ་བྲལ་མ་བྱ་བ། དྲན་པ་ཡོད་ལ་སྙིང་རྗེ་དང་མ་འབྲེལ་བ་ཡིན། དེ་ལ་ཐུན་འགོར་སེམས་ཅན་ཐམས་ཅད་ཀྱི་དོན་དུ་བསྒོམ་མོ་སྙམ་པ་དང་། ཐུན་མཐར་དགེ་བས་སེམས་ཅན་ཐམས་ཅད་སངས་རྒྱས་ཐོབ་པར་གྱུར་ཅིག་པར་བསྔོ། ཨོ་རྒྱན་ཆེན་པོས། སྙིང་རྗེ་མེད་ན་ཆོས་ཀྱི་རྩ་བ་རུལ། ཞེས་གསུངས་པས་གལ་ཤིན་ཏུ་ཆེ། བདག་མེད་མ་བྱ་བསྒོམ་སྐྱེས་ནས་མ་བསྐྱངས་པར་བོར་བ་ལ་ཟེར། བློ་ནང་དུ་ཀུག་ནས་སྒོམ་དུ་བཅུག རེས་འཇོག་མ་བྱ་བ་རེས་སྒོམ་འོང་། རེས་མི་འོང་པ་དེ་ཡིན། དེ་ལ་བྱུང་མ་བྱུང་ཁྱད་མེད་པའི་ཐོག་ཏུ་འཇོག་ཅིང་ཉམས་སུ་བླངས། འཁོར་ཡུག་མ་བྱ་བ་ཉིན་མོའི་དྲན་པ་མཚན་མོ་ཡང་འོང་བ་དེ་ཡིན། འདི་སྒོམ་གྱིས་ཚུར་འཛུས་པའི་དུས་དེ་ཡིན། རྣལ་འབྱོར་མཆོག་ཅེས་པ་རྫོགས་པ་ཆེན་པོ་བྱ་རྩོལ་དང་བྲལ་བའི་དུས་ཞེས་བྱ་བ་དེ་ཡིན། ཕྱག་རྒྱ་ཆེན་པོ་བསྒོམ་མེད་ཟེར་བ་ཡིན་ནོ། ཡང་གང་ཟག་རིགས་ཆད་ཅེས་བ་ཁྲིགས་ཆོད་ཐོད་རྒལ་གྱི་སྣོད་དུ་མ་གྱུར་པ་དག་ཀྱང་ཡོད་པས། དེ་འདྲའི་རིགས་ལ་དབང་བསྐུར་རྩ་རླུང་སྦྱངས་ནས་ལས་ཀྱི་ཕྱག་རྒྱ་གཏད། དབང་པོ་གཉིས་སྦྱོར་གྱིས་དགའ་བཞི་འབྲོས་འདོད་ཀྱིས་བདེ་བའི་ངོ་བོ་སྟོང་པར་ངོ་སྤྲོད་དེ་གོང་བཞིན་སེམས་ཁྲིད་ལ་འཛུག་པར་གསུངས་ལ། དེའང

## Conclusion

This is how the practice methods are taught, divided into the nine parts of the three capabilities of best, average, and lesser. The perspective in the aural lineage of the Great Completion is described thus:

> Best capability can meditate directly with view.
> Average capability can meditate directly with meditation.
> Lesser capability can practice directly with activity.

In any case, one must engender fortitude in meditation. The old adage is certainly true: "Though the Dharma be profound, without meditation the profound instructions are left behind in the scriptures." Even though meditation affects your mind at present, if you do not meditate continually your mind becomes stubborn, and practice becomes stubborn, and it will not help at the time of death. So take care. Gyalwa Götsangpa said that six things are needed:

> Outer retreat is to stay put in isolation.
> Inner retreat is to stay put in the retreat hut.
> Secret retreat is to stay put on the mat.
> Stay put upon the nondual view.
> Stay put upon undistracted meditation.
> Stay put upon unattached conduct.

Generally, in meditation there is both "to take hold" and "to be held."[23] In the mind that is not ready,[24] one needs to take hold of the meditation subject and not lack mindfulness. Then when the thought itself holds you, whatever arises all becomes meditation. Then that becomes a state of no-fixation in ordinary mind itself.

> Though a great meditator gives up meditation,
> Meditation does not give up a great meditator.

To bring that about, you have to meditate continuously. Without meditation, even if a few minor experiences occur now, they will dissipate. This is the "rainbow meditation." "The hook" is when you hold with mindfulness. Without holding, there will be nothing. You must tighten the watch guard

མི་ནུས་པ་ལ་ནི་བཏག་གྲོལ་མཐོང་གྲོལ་མྱོང་གྲོལ་ལ་སོགས་པའི་ཐབས་ཀྱིས་རིམ་གྱིས་གྲོལ་བར་འགྱུར་བའི་ཚུལ་ལ་འཇུག་པར་བྱའོ། སྤྱིར་སེམས་ཕྱོགས་དང་། ཕྱག་ཆེན་པོ་ནི། ཡེ་ཤེས་སྤྱིར་གསལ་ཞེས་བྱ་སྟེ། བརྟན་པ་མ་ཐོབ་བར་དུ་ཡིད་དཔྱོད་འཛིན་པའི་ལྟ་བ་ཞེས་བཤད། འོན་ཀྱང་རྫོགས་ཆེན་པ་དེ་དོ་སྤྱོད་ནས་བསྒོམ་ན་ཕྱི་སྣང་བའི་ཡུལ་དང་། ནང་འཛིན་པའི་སེམས་ཀྱི་འཕྲོ་གནས་ཐམས་ཅད་ཡེ་ཤེས་སུ་འཆར་བས། རྫོགས་ཆེན་རང་སྣང་རིས་མེད་ཀྱི་དགོངས་པ་ཟེར་གཡེར་པོ་ཆེ་བྱེད། གང་ལྟར་རུང་སྟེ། སེམས་ངོ་འཕྲོད་ཕྱིན་ཆད་སྣང་ཐོག་ཏུ་ཉམས་ལེན་སྐྱོང་བ་ལ། ཐོད་རྒལ་ལ་ཞུགས་ཏེ་མུན་ཁྲིད་དམ། སྣང་ཁྲིད་བྱས་ནས་འོད་གསལ་སྟོང་གཟུགས་ཀྱི་ཐོག་ཏུ་ཉམས་ལེན་བསྐྱངས་ན་རང་བྱུང་གི་ཡེ་ཤེས་མངོན་སུམ་དུ་འགྱུར་ཏེ། ཆོས་ཉིད་ཀྱི་བར་དོ་ལ་གྲོལ་བར་ཐེ་ཚོམ་མེད་དོ། བདག་ལྟ་བུའི་བསྒོམ་པའི་ཉམས་མྱོང་མེད་ཅིང་། ཐོས་པ་ཐལ་ཆེར་ཀུང་བརྗོད་པའི་མན་ངག་ལ་མྱོང་བ་མེད་པ་འདི་འདྲ་བ། རྗེ་འབའ་ར་བས། བསྒོམ་པའི་ཉམས་མྱོང་མེད་པའི། ཡིག་ནག་དཔེ་ཆའི་སྟེང་ནས། བསྒོམ་ཁྲིད་འདེབས་བློ་བྱས་ཀྱང་། ལམ་ལོག་གོམ་པར་སྨྲུར་ཏོ། ཞེས་གསུངས་གསུངས་པ་བཞིན་དང་། ཡང་དེས་ས་ཐོབ་ཡོན་ཏན་མེད་ཀྱང་། བཟོད་ཐོབ་ལས་བཞི་འགྲུབ་ཅིང་། སྙིང་རྗེའི་རྩ་བ་བརྟན་པས། འགྲོ་དོན་བྱས་ཀྱང་ཚོག་གོ། ཞེས་གསུངས་པས། བཟོད་པ་མ་ཐོབ་ཀྱང་རུང་རྒྱུད་ལ་སྙིང་རྗེ་ཙུང་ཟད་ཅིག་ཡོད་པ་དང་། ཁྱད་པར་དུ་སེམས་དང་ཆོས་སུ་འདྲེས་ཤིང་། ཏིང་འཛིན་ལས་སུ་རུང་བ་དང་། སངས་རྒྱས་ལྟ་བུའི་བླ་མ་དམ་པ་རྣམས་ཀྱི་གསུང་རྒྱུན་གང་དྲན་བཀོད་པ་ཡིན་ནོ། སློབ་དཔོན་ཤྲཱི་སེང་ཧས། དང་པོ་ཐུག་གར་གཅུག། བར་དུ་འཇོག་སར་ཞོག། ཐ་མ་འགྲོ་སར་ཐོང་གསུངས། དེ་ལ་དང་པོ་ནི་ཁྲིད་སྟོན་ཤེས་པའི་བླ་མ་ལ་གཏུགས་ནས་སེམས་ཀྱི་རྩད་གདར་བཅད་དེ་ཞུན་གཏུག་བྱེད་པའོ། བར་དུ་གང་ཤར་བཟོ་བཅོས་མེད་པར་འཇོག་པའོ། ཐ་མ་ཉམས་མྱོང་

of nondistraction. "Separation of two" is when there is mindfulness but it is not combined with compassion. For that, you should think, "I will meditate for the welfare of all sentient beings" at the start of every session and dedicate at the end of the session with "may all sentient beings attain awakening." The Great Orgyen said, "Without compassion the root of Dharma is rotten." This is extremely important.

"Non-ownership" is to engender meditation and then not maintain it but discard it. Draw the mind inside and enter meditation. "Intermittent placement" means that sometimes the meditation goes well and sometimes not. For that, practice by focusing directly, indifferent to whether it is happening or not. "Around the clock" is when the mindfulness that is applied in the daytime also occurs at night. This is when you are held by meditation.[25] The "sublime yoga" is when one is free from acting and striving in the Great Completion. In the Great Seal it is also called "no meditation."[26]

Moreover, there are the individuals of the "cut-off family" who are not appropriate recipients of trekchö and tögal. Those types should receive empowerments, train in practices of the channels and winds, and focus on the Action Seal. The proper sequence of the four pleasures that arise from the intercourse of the two organs will reveal the essence of bliss as empty. This is said to be entering the mind-guidance as described above. However, those who cannot do it should engage in the ways of gradual liberation through skillful means, such as liberation through wearing, liberation through seeing, and liberation through tasting.

In the general Mind Class of Great Completion and in the Great Seal teachings there is what is called "general clarity of pristine wisdom." It is explained as "the view that holds mental examination until stability is attained."[27] However, for Great Completion practitioners, once there has been the revelation and meditation upon it, all externally appearing objects and the active or still inner mind that grasps them arise as pristine wisdom. This is the famous "perspective of unbiased self-display" of the Great Completion.

In any case, cultivate the practice directly upon appearances from the time that mind has been revealed. When you enter into tögal practice from the dark retreat guidance or appearance guidance, innately occurring pristine wisdom will become manifest when practice is maintained directly upon lucent empty form. Thus liberation in the intermediate stage (Tib. *bar do*) of dharmata is assured.

For someone like me, without meditative experience and even without

ཉིད་དེ་འཛིན་གྱི་རྩོལ་ཞེན་པ་མེད་པར་འཛིན་མེད་དུ་གཏོང་བའོ། རྫོགས་ཆེན་སེམས་སྡེའི་ཁྲིད་ཡིག་ལས་བཏུས་པའོ། ཀུན་ལ་ཕན་པར་ཤོག

༄ གཞན་ཡང་ཞལ་ཤེས་འཕྲོར་བྱ་ནི། ཉམས་རྟགས་སྣ་ཚོགས་སུ་ཤར་བ་བསྒོམས་པའི་ལག་རྗེས་བཟང་རྟོག་གི་མཐུ་བརྟས་པ་ཡིན་ཀྱང་རྟག་པ་མེད་པས་བདེན་འཛིན་མ་ཞུགས་པ་གནད་དུ་ཆེ། དལྟ་གཟུང་དྲན་ལ་མ་ལྟོས་པར་གང་ཤར་རང་གྲོལ་རྗེན་པར་འགྲོ་བ་དེ་དག་རྣམ་དག་ལེགས་པའི་ལམ་དུ་གོ། བླ་མའི་སྐུའི་སྣང་བ་དང་ཡི་དམ་གྱི་བསྐྱེད་རིམ་སོགས་ཀྱང་སྣང་མེད་དུ་ཨ་ལི་རྗེན་ནེ་བའི་ངང་ནས་བཟླས་པ་སོགས་བྱེད་པ་ལས། སྐུའི་སྣང་བ་དེ་དག་སྣང་ལ་རང་བཞིན་མེད་པ་གསལ་ལ་རྟོག་པ་མེད་པ། བདེ་ལ་ཞེན་པ་མེད་པ་སྟེ་མཚན་ཉིད་གསུམ་ལྡན་སྟོང་པ་ཉིད་ཀྱི་རང་གདངས་སུ་མ་བགགས་པར་ས་ལེར་སྣང་བའི་ངང་ནས་བཟླས་བརྗོད་སོགས་གནང་ན་རྩལ་ཆེ་ཞིང་ཆེད་དུ་བླ་མ་སྤྱི་བོར་བསྒོམ་པ་སོགས་མི་དགོས། ལམ་དུས་ཀྱི་ལམ་འབྲས་བུའི་བཞག་མཚམས་ནི། ལམ་གྱི་དུས་སུ་འང་སེམས་ཉིད་རྩ་བྲལ་རིས་མེད་ཁྱབ་གདལ་དེ་གཞི། དེའི་ངང་ལ་བསལ་བཞག་མེད་པར་ཡུལ་མེད་རང་གསལ་དུ་སྐྱོང་བ་དེ་ལམ། དེས་འབྲས་བུའི་རྫོགས་རིམ་གྱི་ལྷ་སྐུ་ཞུ་བདེ་དང་མཚུངས་ལྡན་དུ་རང་ཤར་བ་ནས་ལམ་གྱི་འབྲས་བུའི་གྲངས་སུ་འགྲོ་བ་ཡིན་ནོ། །དེའང་རྫོགས་ཆེན་གྱི་གཞུང་ནས་ངོ་རང་ཐོག་ཏུ་སྤྲད་པ་ཞེས་པ་ནི། དུས་གསུམ་རྟོག་པ་དང་བྲལ་བའི་དལྟའི་ཤེས་པ་ལ་བཅོས་སླད་མ་བྱས་པར་གཉུག་མའི་ངང་དུ་ཨ་ལི་སང་ངེ། ཆམ་བརྡལ་བ་ཉིད་བཙན་ཐབས་སུ་ངོས་བཟུང་ནས་རང་བྱུང་གི་ཡེ་ཤེས་ངོ་སྤྲོད་པ་དང་། ཐག་གཅིག་ཐོག་ཏུ་བཅད་པ་ཞེས་པ་ནི་དྲན་བསམ་སྔ་མ་འགགས། ཕྱི་མ་མ་སྐྱེས། དལྟའི་ཤེས་པ་རྟོག་བཅས་དྲན་བསམ་གྱི་བློ་འགགས་ནས་བཞི་ཆ་གསུམ་བྲལ་གྱི་རིག་པ་སོ་མ་རྣམ་པར་མི་རྟོག་པའི་ཡེ་ཤེས་རིག་

experience of the esoteric instruction that I have heard but mostly forgotten, it is as Lord Barawa[28] said:

> Devoid of meditational experience,
> Feigning meditation instruction
> Based upon the black letters of the scriptures
> Becomes a walk down the wrong road.

And:

> Even without the qualities of attaining the stages,
> Attaining forbearance, and doing the four activities,
> With the firm root of compassion
> One may yet work for the welfare of beings.

Even without attaining forbearance[29] it is appropriate because I have some compassion in my stream of being and especially, having mixed my mind with the Dharma, I am ready for meditative absorption and established in whatever I recall of the teachings of the buddha-like holy gurus. Master Shri Singha said:

> First, reach the meeting point.
> Next, rest in the resting place.
> Finally, let go to where it goes.

That is, first of all meet the guru who knows how to give guidance, minutely investigate the mind, and reach a level of refinement. In the middle, rest in whatever arises without any contrivance or fabrication. Finally, let it go without fixated attachment in the play of experiential meditative absorption.

This is culled from the guidance manuals of the Great Completion Mind Class. May it benefit all.

## Further Tidbits of Advice

Various signs of meditative experience may arise—the handprints of meditation—that result from the force of a positive mind-frame. But since they are not permanent, do not be trapped into clinging to their validity. This is crucial. Now, without regard for mindful holding, whatever arises becomes

གེ། སེང་ངེ། ཡེར་རེ། ཞ་ལེ་བར་གནས་པ་འདི་ཉིད་དོ།། བཞི་ཆ་གསུམ་བྲལ་ཞེས་པ་ནི། འདས་མ་འོངས་ད་ལྟ་བ་སྟེ་རྟོག་བཅས་ཀྱི་དུས་གསུམ་དང་། རྟོག་མེད་ད་ལྟ་བའི་དུས་གསུམ་དྲན་བསམ་གྱིས་བཅོས་སླད་མེད་པའི་སོ་མ་སྟེ་ཆ་བཞི་ལས་རྟོག་བཅས་ཀྱི་དུས་གསུམ་དང་བྲལ་བའི་རྣམ་པར་མི་རྟོག་པའི་དུས་དེ་བཞི་ཆ་གསུམ་བྲལ་ཆོས་སྐུ་བློ་འདས་ཀྱི་དགོངས་པའོ། གདེངས་གྲོལ་ཐོག་ཏུ་བཅའ་ཞེས་པ་ནི། གང་ཤར་གྱི་རང་ངོ་ལ་བཅོས་བསླད་མེད་པར་ཅེར་རེ་བལྟས་ཏེ་དེའི་ངང་ལ་གློད་པས། དྲན་རྟོག་རྗེས་མེད་དུ་ཡལ་བས་རྦ་རླབས་ཆུར་ཐིམ་པ་ལྟར་གང་ཤར་རང་གྲོལ་སྟོང་གཉེན་དང་བྲལ་བའི་ངང་ལ་གདེངས་འཆོས་པའོ།།

༈ །།རྫོགས་ཆེན་སེམས་ཀློང་གཉིས་ཀྱི་གནད་མན་ངག་གི་སྟེར་འདུས་སྟེ། ཀ་དག་གི་ངང་ལ་མཉམ་པར་བཞག་པས། སྣོད་བཅུད་ཀྱི་སྣང་བ་ཐམས་ཅད་སེམས་ཉིད་རང་བྱུང་གི་ཡེ་ཤེས་བརྗོད་བྲལ་ཆོས་སྐུར་ཐག་ཆོད་པས་སེམས་སྡེའི་གནད་འདུ་ལ། དེ་ཉིད་གང་ལའང་བྱ་རྩོལ་བྲལ་བའི་ཆོས་ཉིད་ཀྱི་ཀློང་དུ་ཐག་ཆོད་པས་ཀློང་སྡེ་འདུ། དེའི་ཕྱིར་སེམས་ཀློང་གཉིས་ཀྱི་ཉམས་ལེན་ཐམས་ཅད་མན་ངག་གི་སྡེའི་ཁྲིགས་གཅོད་ཀྱི་ཉམས་ལེན་གྱི་ཡོངས་སུ་འདུས་པས་རྫོགས་པ་ཆེན་པོའི་ལམ་གྱི་མཆོག་རྩེ་མོ་ནི་མན་ངག་གི་སྡེ་སྟེ། འཁོར་འདས་སྤང་བླང་དང་བྲལ་བའི་ཡིན་ལུགས་གནད་ཐོག་ཏུ་འབེབས་པའི་ཐབས་ཀྱིས་བློ་འདས་རང་བྱུང་གི་ཡེ་ཤེས་སྐད་ཅིག་ལ་འཆར་བར་བྱེད་པས། དོན་ལ་ཆོས་ཐམས་ཅད་ཀྱི་ཆོས་ཉིད་རང་གསལ་གྱི་གནས་ལུགས་མངོན་སུམ་དུ་གཏན་ལ་ཕབ་ནས་ཡེ་ཤེས་འོད་གསལ་ལྷུན་གྲུབ་གཞི་གནས་སུ་ངོ་སྤྲོད་པའི་ཐབས་མཆོག་བླ་ན་མེད་པའོ། ཚོགས་དྲུག་གི་སྣང་བ་གང་ཤར་རང་གྲོལ་དུ་ལམ་དུ་འཁྱེར་བ་དང་ལྷ་སྤུགས་སུ་ཀྲུས་བཏབ་པ་གཉིས་སྤུ་མ་ནུས་པ་ཆེ་མོད། འོན་ཀྱང་རང་གྲོལ་གཅིག་མའི་རྩལ་སྣང་ལྷ་སྤུགས་ཀྱི་རང་གདངས་སུ་བྱ་རྩོལ་མེད་པར་ལམ་དུ་ཁྱེར་ཞེས་པ་ཟུང་འབྲེལ་གྱི་ལམ་ཁྱད་པར་ཅན་དུ་

stark innate freedom. Know that those experiences are completely pure, the right path.

Though there is the visualized appearance of the guru's body, creation phase of the yidam, and so forth, it is all just open, stark nonappearance. When you are doing recitation and such within that state, those appearing forms are appearances without intrinsic existence, clarity without thought, and bliss without attachment. With those three characteristics, the natural radiance of emptiness appears vividly without obstruction. If you do recitation and so forth within that state, you do not particularly need to meditate on the guru on the crown of your head and such in order to make it more effective.

As for the configuration of ground, path, and fruition in terms of the path: At the time of the path, the ground is mind-as-such: rootless, unbiased, pervasive. Within that state, the path is maintaining innate clarity without resting in clarity as an object. As a result, the concurrent natural arising of the deity's body and the melting and bliss of completion phase is counted as the fruition of the path.

A classic scripture of the Great Completion[30] teaches "introduction directly to one's own nature." The mind of nowness is free of thoughts of the three times. Within that unadulterated natural state, recognizing the open transparent pervasiveness in a forthright manner reveals the innately occurring pristine wisdom.

"Decide directly upon one thing" means that while the previous thought has ceased and the next one has not yet arisen, in that mind of nowness when the mind of conceptual thought ceases and the intrinsic awareness is free of three parts out of four, you abide in fresh, totally nonconceptual pristine wisdom—wakeful, vibrant, immaculate openness. It is this very thing. "Free of three parts out of four" refers to past, future, and present, the three times of conceptual thinking, and to the nonconceptual present, that freshness uncorrupted by thoughts of the three times. So of these four times, it is the totally nonconceptual time that is free of the three conceptual times. That is known as "free of three parts out of four." It is the perspective of dharmakaya beyond intellect.

"To have confidence directly in liberation" means to look nakedly at whatever arises without corrupting it, and then relax into that state. By that, the thoughts will disappear without a trace like the swells subsiding in the sea. Have confidence in whatever arises as innately liberated, without rejecting it or using a remedy.

འགྲོ་བ་ལགས།། རིག་པ་རྗེན་པར་འཆར་སྒོ་སྣ་ཚོགས་སུ་འཆར་ཡང་གང་ཤར་ཐམས་ཅད་དྲན་པ་ཁོ་རང་ལས་མ་གཡོས་པ་གཟུང་དྲན་ལ་མ་ལྟོས་པར་སྐྱོང་ཐུབ་པ་དེ། རྫོགས་ཆེན་པའི་ལུགས་ལ་ཉམས་ཀྱི་སྐྱེ་རིམ་བཞི་ལས་གནས་པའི་ཉམས་དང་། ཕྱག་ཆེན་པའི་ལུགས་ཀྱི་རྩེ་གཅིག་ཏུ་གནས་པ་ཕྱོགས་འདྲ་བས་སེམས་ཀྱི་ངོ་བོའི་ཕྱོགས་མཐོང་ཙམ་ལོས་ཡིན། འོན་ཀྱང་བརྟན་པ་ཐོབ་མ་ཐོབ་ཙམ་ལས་འདི་བས་ལྷག་པ་ཞིག་མཐོང་རྒྱུ་འམ་རྟོགས་རྒྱུ་མེད་དམ་སྙམས་པ་དེ། ཡིན་ལུགས་གང་མཐུན་པའི་གོ་མྱོང་གི་ཆ་ནས་བློ་མ་འཁྲུལ་པའི་ཡེ་ཤེས་འདྲ་ཡང་། འདི་ལས་ལྷག་པ་མེད་དམ་སྙམ་པའི་ཆོས་ཀྱི་བདག་འཛིན་གྱི་བློ་དང་བཅས་པའི་རྣམ་རྟོག་ཅན་དུ་འགྱུར་བས། རང་གི་རིག་པ་ལ་རྗེན་ཅེར་བལྟས་པའི་དུས་ཀྱི་གཤིས་སྦྱོར་བྲལ་བློས་གང་དུ་ཡང་གཟུང་དུ་མེད་པ་དེ་དང་། གོ་བའི་སྟོང་ཉིད་གཉིས་ལ་མྱོང་ལུགས་མི་འདྲ་མཁྱེན་དགོས། འོན་ཀྱང་སེམས་ཀྱི་ངོ་བོ་མཐོང་བ་ཞེས་པ་ཡང་དོན་སྤྱི་ཙམ་མཐོང་བའི་དཔེའི་ཡེ་ཤེས་ལ་རང་ངོ་སྤྲོད་པའི་ཐབས་མཁས་ལས། རང་རིག་པའི་ཡེ་ཤེས་རྣམ་པར་མི་རྟོག་པའི་ངོ་བོ་རང་མཚན་པ་ནི་འཕགས་པའི་ས་ཐོབ་ནམ་གཏོགས་སྒོམ་བྱུང་ལ་རང་དབང་འབྱོར་བའི་སྦྱོར་ལམ་ངེས་འབྱེད་ཀྱི་དུས་སུ་འང་མེད་ན་ཚོགས་ལམ་པ་དང་ལམ་མ་ཞུགས་ཀྱི་བསམ་གཏན་པའི་རྒྱུད་ལ་ལྟ་ཅི་སྨོས། དེས་ན་ཤན་ཕྱེད་དགོས། རྨི་ལམ་རང་ངོ་ཤེས་པའི་དྲན་པའི་ངང་ནས་རྩལ་སྦྱོང་དང་རྨི་ལམ་མོ་སྙམ་པའི་དྲན་ཤེས་མེད་པར་རྩལ་སྦྱོང་ཉིན་མོ་ལས་གསལ་དྭངས་ཆེ་བ་ཡོད་པ་དེ་རྨི་ལམ་ཟིན་སྦྱོང་སྤྲུལ་སྒྱུར་གྱི་ངོས་ནས་སྔ་མ་མི་འགྱུར་ཞིང་བརྟན་ལ་ཕྱིས་བོགས་ཆེ། ཕྱི་མ་དེ་ཉིན་མོའི་དགེ་སྦྱོར་གྱི་ཤུགས་ཀྱིས་སླེབ་པའི་ཉམས་སྣང་ཙམ་དུ་ཟད་པས་རྨི་ལམ་ཟིན་སྦྱོང་བརྟན་ཆགས་ཀྱི་གནད་དུ་འགྲོ་བ་ཉུང་། ཕལ་ནས་གཉིད་འཐུག་གི་སྐབས་སུ་གསལ་སྟོང་གི་རིག་པ་རྣམ་རྟོག་གི་གཡའ་དང་བྲལ་ཞིང་རང་ངོ་སྐྱོང་ཐུབ་པ། དེའི་རྩལ་སྣང་རྨི་ལམ་གྱི་སྤྲུལ་བསྒྱུར་དུ་ལྡང་ཐུབ་པ་ཞིག་

The crucial points of both the Mind Class and the Space Class of the Great Completion are contained in the Esoteric Instruction Class. In meditative equipoise within primordial purity, all appearances of the world and beings are determined to be mind-as-such,[31] innately occurring pristine wisdom, the indescribable dharmakaya. That summarizes the crucial point of the Mind Class. Determining that itself as being the space of true being, altogether free of effortful action, summarizes the Space Class. Therefore, all the practices of the Mind and Space sections are contained in the trekchö practices of the Esoteric Instruction Class. Thus the pinnacle of the sublime path of Great Completion is the Esoteric Instruction Class. The method of hitting directly on the crucial point of reality without rejecting or accepting samsara or nirvana instantly arouses the innately occurring pristine wisdom beyond intellect. This means that it is the supreme sublime method that manifestly confirms the innate clear nature of the true being of all phenomena, and thus reveals the spontaneously present clear light pristine wisdom that abides as the basic ground.

Of these two—integrating the innate freedom of whatever arises to the six sense groups into the spiritual path and applying the seal of deity and mantra to those appearances—the former is certainly more effective. Yet to know how to integrate effortlessly on the path the dynamic appearance of the innately free natural state as the natural radiance of deity and mantra is indeed the special approach of unity.

Various experiences arise in stark awareness, yet whatever arises does not shift from mindfulness itself and can be maintained without depending on mindful holding. This is basically similar to the "abiding experience" of the four stages of experience in the Great Completion tradition and the "one-pointed abiding" of the Great Seal tradition in that there is certainly a glimpse in the direction of mind's essence. However, you may think that other than just the attainment or lack of stability, there is no special thing to be seen or realized other than this. In terms of personal understanding of reality in an appropriate way, mind is similar to undeluded awareness. But if you wonder about whether there is not something more, it becomes the conceptuality of intellectual clinging to the identity of phenomena. When you look nakedly and starkly at innate awareness, that basic character is free of embellishment with no clinging whatsoever. That and the emptiness that is merely understood are two different ways of experiencing. You must understand this.

Moreover, the phrase "to see the essence of mind" refers to merely the

ཀྱང་འབྱུང་སྟེ། གཉིད་ཀྱི་འོད་གསལ་ཟིན་པའི་གྲངས་སུ་འགྲོ་ཞིང་། དེ་འདྲ་དེ་རྨི་ལམ་དུ་ཡངས་ནས་ཀྱང་རྨི་ལམ་དུས་ཀྱི་དྲན་ཤེས་ཀྱིས་མ་ཟིན་འདང་གནད་དུ་འགྲོ། ཐོད་རྒྱལ་གྱི་དུས་སྟོང་གཟུགས་ཀྱི་རྟགས་སྣང་ལ་ལྟ་སྟང་གྱི་ལམ་ནས་དྭངས་ཏེ་རྣམ་པར་རྟོག་མེད་ཀྱི་ངང་དུ་འཇོག་པ་དེ་ལ་གོམས་པས་ཞི་གནས་ཙམ་ལས་སོ་སོར་རྟོག་པའི་ཤེས་རབ་ཀྱི་དཔྱད་པ་མེད་པས་ལྷག་མཐོང་མི་འགྲོ་བར་སླུམས་མཁན་མང་ནའང་། རྣམ་པར་མི་རྟོག་པའི་ཏིང་ངེ་འཛིན་ལ་གོམས་པ་ལས་མི་རྟོག་པའི་ཡེ་ཤེས་སྐྱེས་པར་གྱུར་པ་དེ་ཀ་སོ་སོར་རྟོག་པའི་ཤེས་རབ་ཀྱི་ལྷག་མཐོང་སྐྱེས་པ་ཡིན་པར་དུས་འཁོར་སོགས་ལས་ཀྱང་བཤད་ཅིང་། ཁྱད་པར་རྫོགས་པ་ཆེན་པོ་རང་གི་ལུགས་ལ། ལུས་བཞུགས་སྟངས། མིག་ལྟ་སྟངས། རླུང་མི་འགྱུལ་བ་གསུམ་ལ་གཞི་བཅས་པས་རིམ་པར་རྩ་རླུང་ལ་གནད་དུ་བསྣུན་པས་རྣམ་རྟོག་འགགས། མངོན་སུམ་ཡུལ་ལ་གསལ་བས་ཡིད་དཔྱོད་ཚིག་གི་སྒྲོ་འདོགས་དང་བྲལ། ཆོས་ཉིད་རང་ངོར་གནས་པས་མ་བུ་འདྲེས་ཏེ་གདོད་མའི་དབྱིངས་སུ་ལ་ཟློ་བ་ཡིན་པས་ཐིག་ལེ་ལུ་གུ་རྒྱུད་བཅས་པའི་རྟགས་སྣང་ལ་ལྟ་སྟངས་ཀྱིས་ཅེར་རེ་གཏད་དེ། རྟགས་སྣང་དེ་ཁའི་རང་བཞིན་ཧྲིག་གེ་བའི་ངང་ལ་བཟོ་མེད་ཡེངས་མེད་དུ་འཇོག་པ་ལོ་ནས་གནད་དུ་འགྲོ་བ་ལགས། ཆོས་ཉིད་བར་དོའི་སྐབས་ཀྱི་བསམ་གཏན་གྱི་ཞག་གི་ཚད་མཉམ་རྗེས་འདྲེས་ནས་ཏིང་ངེ་འཛིན་ཐུན་ཚོད་ལས་འདས་པ་ཡེ་ཤེས་ལྷུན་གྲུབ་ཀྱི་ཉམས་སྐྱེས་པ་ལ་མཐའ་འདི་ཙམ་ཞེས་ཚོད་འཛིན་དཀའ་མོད། སྤྱི་ཙམ་དུ་བསམ་གཏན་ལ་མཉམ་པར་བཞག་པས་རྣམ་རྟོག་གིས་བར་མ་ཆོད་པར་ཇི་ཙམ་གནས་པའི་ཡུན་དེ་ཙམ་དུ་འཇོག ཆོས་ཉིད་བར་དོར་དེ་གྲོལ་ནུས་ཀྱི་ཚད་འོད་གསལ་སྣང་བ་བཞི་ལ་ད་ལྟ་ནས་རང་བྱན་ཆུད་པ་ཞིག་གལ་ཆེ་བས་རྨི་ལམ་གྱི་ཉམས་ལེན་ཚད་དུ་སོང་མ་སོང་གིས་འཛིན་པ་ལགས། མཉམ་བཞག་གི་ངོར་འཕྲོ་བར་སྣང་ཡང་དྲན་པ་ཁོར་འཁྱོངས་ཙམ་བདེ་གསལ་གྱི་ཉམས་དང་བཅས་ཤར་བ་དེ་ལ་

general seeing of symbolic pristine wisdom that is skillfully introduced. Other than that, the authentic essence of totally nonconceptual pristine wisdom of natural intrinsic awareness is realized only by those who have attained the level of noble ones. If even those who have applied total control in meditation results and reached ascertainment on the path of application do not have it, then no need to talk about those meditators on the path of accumulation or those who have not entered the path at all. Therefore these need to be differentiated.

There is a training to practice within the state of mindful recognition of dreams and a training without the mindful awareness of thinking "it's a dream" that brings greater clarity than in the daytime practices. In terms of recognizing, refining, increasing, and changing your dreams, when the former training is ineffective, the latter one will greatly enhance the stability of the practice. Mere appearances of experience occur as a consequence of daytime virtuous practices. Since they will be exhausted, there will be little effect on the vital points of developing stability in recognizing and refining dreams. Usually, it is during the time of deep sleep that clear, empty intrinsic awareness is free of the tarnish of conceptual thought and you can maintain its true nature. From its dynamic appearance comes the ability to arouse the emanations and transformations of dreams. It can then be counted as recognizing the clear light of sleep. If that is the case, then when you arise in the dream, even if you do not recognize it with mindfulness during dreamtime, it is still effective.[32]

At the time of tögal, many people think that remaining in and habituating to a state of nonthought in regard to the appearing signs of empty form that are drawn from deity appearance is merely calm abiding and not the discernment of discriminating intelligence, so it is not considered superior insight. However, it is explained in the Kalachakra Tantra and others that nonconceptual pristine wisdom is born from habituating to absorption without conceptual thought, and just that is the birth of the superior insight of discriminating intelligence.

In particular, in the tradition of Great Completion itself, with the three unmoving states[33] of the physical postures, visual gazes, and winds as the basis, gradually the channels and winds will reach the crucial point and discursive thought will cease. Since it is the field of actual clear perception, there is freedom from the added designations of discernment. Abiding in the nature of true being, mother and child combine. Since this is the decisive leap into the original expanse, unblinkingly focusing with the visual

སྒྲོང་བྱ་སྒྲོང་འདོད་ཀྱི་འཛིན་པ་མ་ཞུགས་ན་གནད་དུ་འགྲོ། གང་ཤར་རང་སེམས་སུ་ཐག་ཆོད་ཅིང་སེམས་ཉིད་རྩ་བྲལ་གསལ་སྟོང་འཛིན་མེད་དུ་ཤར་བས་མཉམ་བཞག་གི་ངོ་ནས་ལུས་སྣང་སེམས་སོགས་ཐ་དད་དུ་འཛིན་པ་རང་དག་ནས་ཕྱི་ནང་བར་མེད་ཧྲར་སང་རྗེན་པར་གནས་པས་རྣམ་རྟོག་རང་ག་མ་མི་འཆང་ལ། ཤར་ཡང་ངོ་ཤེས་ཙམ་གྱིས་ཆོག་པར་སྣང་བ་དེ། སྣང་སེམས་འདྲེས་ཏེ་སྣང་བ་སྒོམ་དུ་ཤར་ཤར་འདྲ་ཡང་ད་དུང་སྟོང་ཉིད་གཟུང་དྲན་མ་ལ་ལྟོས་དགོས་མི་དགོས་ཤན་འབྱེད་དགོས་པས། སྣང་རིག་སོ་མ་འདི་རང་རིག་རང་གསལ་ལ་རྩོལ་སྒྲུབ་དང་དགག་སྒྲུབ་བྲལ་བ་ཞིག་བྱུང་ན་སྣང་བ་སྒོམ་དུ་ཤར་བས་གཟུང་དྲན་ལ་རག་མ་ལུས་ལགས། དེས་ན་རྩོལ་བཅས་ཀྱང་འཛིན་པ་མ་ཞུགས་གང་ཤར་རང་གྲོལ་གྱ་ཡངས་སུ་འཆར་ན་གནད་དུ་འགྲོ་ཞིང་། ལར་ནི་ཅིག་བཞག་གསུམ་གྱིས་རང་གི་དགེ་སྦྱོར་རྒྱུན་བསྐྱངས་ཏེ་དེ་རྟོགས་པའི་ངོ་བོ་ལ་ཅེར་གྲོལ་གྱིས་བལྟས་ནས། ཕྱི་ཆོས་ཅན་ལ་བལྟས་པས་འཁྲུལ་སྣང་བདེན་མེད་དུ་སྣང་བ་སྒྱུ་མ་ལྟ་བུར་རྟོགས་པའི་ངང་ལ་ཞེན་འཛིན་མེད་པར་སྐྱོད། ནང་ཆོས་ཉིད་ལ་བལྟས་པས་ཡུལ་མེད་ནམ་མཁའ་ལྟ་བུར་རྟོགས་པའི་ངང་ལ་འཛིན་མེད་དུ་སྐྱོད། གསང་བ་རིག་པའི་ངོ་བོ་ལ་བལྟས་པས་སྟོང་གསལ་འགགས་མེད་དུ་རྟོགས་ནས་དེའི་ངང་རྩོལ་སྒྲུབ་མེད་པར་སྐྱོད་དེ་མཉམ་པར་བཞག་པས་གནས་སྐབས་སུ་སྤྱན་དང་མངོན་ཤེས་སོགས་ཡོན་ཏན་དཔག་ཏུ་མེད་པ་ལ་རང་དབང་བསྒྱུར་ནུས་ཤིང་ཉོན་མོངས་པ་རང་སར་གྲོལ་བ་ལ་དཀའ་ཚེགས་མེད། དེའང་ལས་དང་པོ་དང་ཡོངས་སུ་སྦྱང་བ་བྱས་པ་དང་། གོམས་པ་ཀློང་དུ་ཕྱུར་པའི་ཡོན་ཏན་རྣམས་སྐྱེ་རིམ་གྱིས་འཕེལ་ནས་སངས་རྒྱས་ཀྱི་ཡེ་ཤེས་འགྲུབ་པའི་ཐབས་ཟབ་མོར་འགྲོ་ཞེས་རྗེ་བླ་མ་དམ་པའི་ཞལ་ནས་མང་དུ་ཐོས་ཤིང་གསུང་དེ་ལ་ཡིད་ཆེས་ཀྱིས་ཚད་མར་བཟུང་ནས་གཞན་ལའང་འདོམས་པ་ལགས་པས་ཐུགས་ལ་བཅག་འཚལ། ལྟ་བའི་ངོ་བོ་གཉིས་ཆོས་སུ་སྣང་བ་ཐམས་ཅད་སོ་སོར་མ་

gazes on the appearing signs of spheres with vajra chains, rest without distraction or fabrication within the transparent nature of those appearing signs themselves. Only through this does it become effective.

During the dharmata intermediate state, the measure of a day of meditative stability is difficult to determine. Once you integrate sitting meditation and postmeditation, the arising of the experience of spontaneously present pristine wisdom goes beyond an allotted period for meditative absorption. So you cannot say just where it ends. But to generalize, while sitting in meditative stability, however long you stay without interruption from discursive thought is how long you have meditated.

It is important to know that the potential for your ability to be liberated in the dharmata during the four visions of clear light is present in you now. You can certainly determine this by whether or not the practice of dreams has measured up.

Even though mental activity arises in the face of meditative equipoise, if you can just barely carry through with mindfulness, it arises endowed with the bliss-clarity experience. If you do not fall into clinging to that experience or the desire for experience, then it will become effective.

With the absolute conviction that whatever arises is your own mind, mind-as-such—rootless, clear, and empty—arises without fixation. In the face of sitting meditation, body, appearance, mind, and all fixation on distinctions are naturally purified and you dwell in stark wakeful openness without outside, inside, or in between, without holding on to regular conceptual thoughts. Though they arise, merely recognize them and let them appear. That is the combining of appearance and mind. Though appearances seem to arise as meditation, from this point on you have to differentiate whether or not you need to depend upon the mindful holding of emptiness. When it happens that this fresh appearing awareness arises as innate aware clarity free of attempts to achieve or stop something, then appearance has arisen as meditation and indeed there is no longer any need of mindful holding. Therefore even with effort, if you do not fall into fixation, whatever occurs arises in the expansiveness of innate freedom and it has become effective.

Again, cultivate the continuity of virtuous practice by the threefold "freely resting."[34] Look at the essence of the ensuing realization with directly liberating perception. Outwardly, looking at conditioned phenomena, you can relax without attachment or fixation in the state of realizing that the deluded appearances appear without validity, like an illusion. Inwardly, looking at true being, you can relax without attachment or fixation in the

དམིགས་པར་རང་རིག་ཡེ་གྲོལ་ལྷུན་གྲུབ་སྟོང་གསལ་སྤྲོས་བྲལ་རྒྱ་ཆད་ཕྱོགས་ལྷུང་བྲལ་བ་དུ་མ་རོ་གཅིག་ཏུ་རྟོགས་པས་ཅི་ལའང་ཡ་ང་བག་ཚ་མེད་པར་སྣང་ཡང་། ཡུལ་ལ་བརྟེན་ནས་ཆགས་སྡང་སོགས་འཆར་འཆར་འདྲ་བ་བྱུང་བ་བདག་འཛིན་གྱི་བློ་མ་ཞུབ་ཀྱི་བར་ལྟ་བའི་གོ་ཡུལ་བཟང་ཡང་སྤྱོད་ཐོག་ཏུ་དེ་དང་འགལ་བ་ལྟར་སྣང་བའང་ཆོས་ཉིད་པས། དེ་ཆེ་གང་ཤར་རང་གྲོལ་ལ་རྫེན་པར་ལམ་དུ་ཁྱེར་བས་གནད་དུ་འགྲོ། དེས་ན་གྲུབ་མཐའི་རྟོག་དཔྱོད་དང་། ཞེན་པའི་སྣང་ཡུལ་དང་། ཡིད་ཀྱི་སྤྱོད་ཡུལ་ལས་འདས་པའི་རང་བཞིན་མཐའ་གྲོལ་ཀློང་ཡངས་ཆེན་པོར་ཡེ་ནས་གནས་པ་ལྟར་དེའི་ངང་བསྐྱངས་པ་གནད་དུ་ཡིན། གང་ལྟར་ཡང་དབྱེར་དུས་ཀྱིས་གཞི་ལ་མྱུ་གུ་གང་ཡང་སྐྱེ་བ་ལྟར་རྣལ་འབྱོར་པའི་ཉམས་ལ་མཐོ་དམན་མཐའ་གཅིག་ཏུ་མ་ངེས་པའི་བཟང་རྟོག་ངན་རྟོག་གིས་བསྡུས་པའི་རྟོག་པའི་རི་མོ་ལྟ་ཅི་སྣོམས། མི་རྟོག་པའི་རང་གདངས་ཀྱི་རྩལ་ལ་མཐའ་དང་བྲལ་བའི་ལྟ་བ། གཉེན་པོས་མ་བཅིངས་པའི་སྒོམ་པ། གང་ཤར་རང་གྲོལ་དུ་གཏོང་བའི་སྤྱོད་པ། རེ་དོགས་གཉིས་འཛིན་དང་བྲལ་བའི་འབྲས་བུའི་སྣང་བ་གང་ཤར་ཡང་སྤྱོད་འདོད་ཀྱི་བློ་ཞུགས་ན་སྨན་མ་ཞུ་བ་དུག་ཏུ་སོང་བ་དང་འདྲ་བས། དེའི་ཆེ་ཐག་ཆོད་པའི་དོན་དེ་ཁའི་ངང་ལ་འཛིན་ཞེན་གྱིས་མ་བཅིངས་པར་མ་ཡེངས་མི་སྒོམ་པའི་རང་འགྲོས་ཀྱིས་རྟག་ཏུ་འཚོ་བར་མཛད་ན་འཚོངས་པ་ལགས། སྟི་ལམ་རགས་པ་རྟག་ཏུ་ཟིན་པ་འདྲ་བ་དེའང་ཟིན་ཙམ་གྱིས་མི་ཆོག ད་དུང་ཉིན་སྣང་ཚོགས་དྲུག་གི་སྣང་བ་ལ་འཛིན་པ་མ་ཞུགས་པར་འབད་རྩོལ་གྱིས་འཆུན་པར་མཛད་ནས་གཉིད་དུ་འགྲོ་དུས་ཉིན་པར་གྱི་དྲན་ཤུགས་ཤོར་བར་གཉིད་ལོག་པས་ཉམས་དང་རྟོགས་པ་འོད་གསལ་རྣམས་རིམ་པར་འཆར་བ་ཡིན་ནོ། ཉམས་གང་ལྟར་སྐྱེས་ཀྱང་དགག་སྒྲུབ་དང་བླང་དོར་གྱི་རྟོག་པས་མ་བསླད་པར་གང་ཤར་གྱི་རང་ངོ་བསྐྱངས་པས་གཟུང་འཛིན་གྱི་རྟོག་ཚོགས་ནམ་མཁའ་ལ་སྤྲིན་དེངས་པ་ལྟར་སངས་ཤིང་འཁོར་བའི་ས་བོན་ཟད་དེ།

state of realizing objectlessness, like the sky. Secretly, looking at the essence of intrinsic awareness and realizing emptiness, clarity, and unimpededness, you can relax without effort in that state.

The immediate benefit from that meditative equipoise is to be in complete control of immeasurable qualities such as the "eyes" and clairvoyances, and the afflictive emotions will be freed in their own ground without difficulty. The qualities that arise from the initial thorough training and subsequent actualization will gradually increase and become a profound method of accomplishing buddha-wisdom. This I heard many times directly from my true Lord Guru. Thus, with confidence, I hold it to be the truth. And since others also advise thus, keep it in your heart.

The essence of the view is the realization of intrinsic awareness, without individual reference to all dualistic phenomena, as free since forever, spontaneously present, empty, clear, unembellished, vast, unbiased, and the single flavor of the multitude. Then anything at all can appear without worry or anxiety. However, until the mind of self-fixation subsides, when something like anger or desire seems to arise in response to objects, even though the theoretical view is excellent, the direct experience may appear in contradiction to it. This is natural. So when that happens, you should directly integrate the natural freedom of whatever arises into the path and it will become effective.

Therefore, the crucial point is just to maintain the state, as if abiding since forever in the great wide vast expanse which is naturally free of limitations, transcending the investigations of philosophical schools, the objective appearances of attachment, and mental operations. In any case, just like anything might sprout from the ground in summertime, the experiences of a yogin might be high or low—they are not all of one type. There is no need to even mention the overall thought patterns that include good and bad thoughts.

The view is free of limitation, the expression of the natural radiance of nonthought. The meditation is not bound up with antidotes. The conduct is letting whatever arises be in its natural freedom. The fruition is free of the dualistic fixation on hopes and fears.

If you fall into the mind-frame of desiring to experience whatever appearance arises, then it has become like medicine that does not dissolve and turns to poison. So at that time remain in the state of total conviction without getting bound up by fixation and attachment. You will be well satisfied if you always proceed at the natural pace of undistracted nonmeditation.

དབྱིངས་རང་བཞིན་གྱིས་རྣམ་པར་དག་པའི་ཀློང་དུ་རིག་པ་རང་བཞིན་གྱིས་རྣམ་པར་དག་པ་ཐིམ་པས་མ་བུ་འདྲེས་ནས་གཟུང་འཛིན་གཉིས་མེད་ཀྱི་ཡེ་ཤེས་འགྱུར་མེད་ཀྱི་དབྱིངས་སུ་གནས་ལ་ཕེབས་ཏེ། ཐ་སྣབས་ཆུར་ཐིམ་པ་བཞིན་དུ་རྣམ་རྟོག་དབྱིངས་སུ་དག་པས་འཁོར་འདས་ཀྱི་བར་ལག་འགྲེལ། ལམ་ལྔ་ས་བཅུ་རིམ་གྱིས་ལམ་ཅིག་ཅར་དུ་བགྲོད་དེ་གྲོལ་བར་འགྱུར་རོ།། །།

Though you may always recognize your obvious dreams, just recognizing them is not enough. Henceforth, having purposely tamed the appearances of the six consciousness groups in the daytime without falling into fixation, when it is time to go to sleep, fall asleep without losing the force of the daytime mindfulness. Then the progression of experience and realization of the clear light will arise.

Whatever kinds of experiences occur, do not corrupt them with thoughts of practicing or preventing, accepting or rejecting. Rather, remain in the face of whatever arises. The hosts of dualistic thought clear away like the dispersed clouds in the sky, and the seed of cyclic existence is exhausted. In the expanse of naturally pure space, naturally pure intrinsic awareness dissolves and mother and child combine. Then unchanging nondualistic pristine wisdom is transcribed in space. Like waves dissolving into water, thoughts are purified into the expanse, and the gap between samsara and nirvana collapses. The five paths and ten levels are traversed all at once, and you are free.

Guru Padmasambhava and Yeshe Tsogyal

# The Dzogchen Instructions of Aro Yeshe Jungne

*A Teaching by Khenchen Palden Sherab Rinpoche and Khenpo Tsewang Dongyal Rinpoche*

# 1: Aro Yeshe Jungne and His Legacy

Aro Yeshe Jungne is renowned as one of the great high-capability practitioners in history because the moment he received the Dzogchen teaching, he practiced it and became enlightened on the spot. Following his enlightenment, he gave essence instructions to others. The Aro teachings became very famous. By practicing them, many people reached enlightenment, and some attained the transcendental wisdom rainbow body. His teachings became known as *Aro Trigey Chemo:* "Aro's Grand (or Great) Dzogchen Teachings." They were also known as *Aro Chogya Chemo*, which means "Aro's Grand Teachings on Abiding in the Dzogchen State." The essence of Aro's teaching is how to identify the nature of the mind, how to abide in it as a way of life, and how to liberate turbulent thoughts and emotions if and when they arise.

Aro Yeshe Jungne appeared during the tenth century, in eastern Tibet, in Kham, in the area called Lhongting Drolma. We will talk about the unusual circumstances in which he was discovered—there is no record of his actual birth—and also a bit about his early days, but first we will discuss the spiritual significance of Lhongting Drolma.

In ancient times Dharma King Songtsen Gampo, a renowned emanation of Avalokiteshvara and King Trisong Deutsen's great-great-great grandfather, built a temple on each one of the 108 geomantic power places throughout the vast Tibetan territory. Some of the sites were near the borders of China and Nepal; some were close to the Silk Road near Turkestan, or Leggo, as it was known to Tibetans at that time. Lhongting Drolma, in the east, was one of those 108 power places; it was also the location of a famous statue of Tara. This statue was blessed by Songtsen Gampo himself, as well as by other masters.

In Lhongting Drolma there was a river of spring water. One day a nun saw a baby lying on its back on the ground near that river. The baby was looking at the sky, saying, "AH, AH, AH." This nun observed that the baby was newly born; she felt compassion for him and thought, "If this baby is left alone it will die. But if I take him, as I am a nun, people will assume the worst and gossip about me. I should go immediately and find help." She left the baby, and hurried to a wealthy local family. She urged them to look after the baby.

The head of the family went there at once. He picked up the baby, took him home, and assisted by other family members, took care of him. Then he searched for the baby's parents. But he could not find them; in fact, they were never located. In the meantime, in his new home, the baby was always pleasant and happy. He never cried. He just stayed lying on his back, saying, "AH, AH, AH." The family adopted him and named him "Aro"—"AH" for his favorite sound, and "*ro*," which means "corpse," for his favorite position.

Near that area, two centuries earlier, Trisong Deutsen built twelve academic institutes and twelve meditation retreat centers. At this time only one academic institute was still functioning. When Aro was able to walk he asked his parents if he could go there. His parents gave him permission. He arrived at the institute and was greeted by a number of monks. "I came here to do practice," Aro said. "You are too young, Aro, and cannot do what is necessary to stay," the monks replied. "I *can* do what is necessary, and I want to stay," he insisted. "But you do not know Dharma," they said. Aro replied, "I know many Dharmas. What Dharmas do you know?" The monks mentioned various texts they had been studying. "What are you studying now?" Aro asked. "We are studying Shantideva's *Guide to the Bodhisattva's Way of Life*. Do you know it?" "Yes, I know it."

The monks brought out the text, handed it to him, and said, "Read it aloud and tell us what it means." Aro read the text and explained the meaning. The monks were very impressed. Then Aro said, "I also know some Dharmas that you do not." He proceeded to give the monks Dzogchen Semde teachings. They were astonished, and said, "Truly, Aro is the source of wisdom." "Source of wisdom" in Tibetan is *yeshe jungne*. He kept the name he received from his family, and to that added the name he received from the monks and in this way became Aro Yeshe Jungne. Later the monks asked him, "How is it that you are so learned?" "I have been studying with Vairochana and Jnana Kumara," he replied. This was amazing, because Vairochana and Jnana Kumara, both of whom were famous translators and students of Guru Padmasambhava, Shantarakshita, and Vimalamitra, lived two centuries before Aro Yeshe Jungne.

Following his stay in the monastery, for many years Aro, even though he was already enlightened, continued to meet teachers in living lineage style. He became a renowned Dzogchen teacher, benefiting many beings. Many persons came from eastern, northern, and central Tibet to receive his teachings. Two lineages developed. One is as follows:

1. Aro Yeshe Jungne
2. Yazi Bonton of Kham
3. Drulsha Gyalpo of Kharab
4. Drumshig Sherab Monlam of Wu
5. Chogro Sangkar of Tsam
6. Rongzom Chokyi Zangpo

The sixth lineage holder, Rongzom Chokyi Zangpo, also known as Rongzompa, was a great master who held all the Nyingma kama lineages. He incorporated the Aro teachings into the Nyingma kama. As a result, as the Nyingma kama flowed through the centuries into the present day, naturally the Aro teachings flowed with it.

Aro's direct student Yazi Bonton of Kham went to the center of Tibet and transmitted his master's teachings in that location. A second lineage developed:

1. Aro Yeshe Jungne
2. Yazi Bonton of Kham
3. Drugu Longjung
4. Bagom Sonam Gyaltsen
5. Tsangrong Dampa Zingum
6. Paragomchen of Yardrog
7. Jomo Myangmo of Yuchu
8. Lharje Lhakangpa of Chokhar
9. Tonpa Shayah of Wu
10. Shigpo Dudtsi

In particular, the fourth of these lineage holders, Bagom Sonam Gyaltsen, discussed his realization of the true nature as well as the Aro teachings with the great Kadam master Atisha; the latter was very pleased. Then Atisha said to Bagom, "If you unite aspiration prayers of loving-kindness and compassion to the Aro teachings, if you ever have trouble with your practice,

Maitreya and Avalokiteshvara will come to your aid." Bagom did as Atisha suggested, and from that time on, the hallmark of this second Aro lineage was the fusion of Kadam teachings stemming from Atisha with the Dzogchen Semde instructions of Aro Yeshe Jungne.

One of Bagom's disciples was Karab Longjong, who was contemporaneous with the great master Sakya Pandita. There is a very interesting story that involves Karab Longjong. At this time—it was the thirteenth century—the Mongolian emperor Godan Khan ruled most of Asia. Godan Khan wrote a letter to Sakya Pandita saying, "Under the sky and on the earth, I am the most powerful man alive. I do not have to ask anyone for anything regarding this life. But I am vexed about the next life. I have looked into spiritual matters and have sought out teachers from all the spiritual schools on this earth. Among all these schools, Buddhism makes the most sense to me. Among all the schools of Buddhism on this earth, Tibetan Buddhism makes the most sense to me. I am told that of all the Tibetan Buddhist masters, you, Sakya Pandita, are the greatest. Therefore I want to meet you. Shall I come to you or will you come to me? If I come to you the Tibetan people will suffer. If you come to me no one will suffer. The choice is yours." So Sakya Pandita came.

Godan Khan asked Sakya Pandita, "Who is the most successful person in Tibet? Who is the richest? Who is the best speaker?" Sakya Pandita answered, "I am the best speaker in Tibet. The richest person is Karab Longjong. And the most successful is Milarepa." The histories say that Godan Khan sent messengers to Tibet to check whether or not this was true. The messengers observed that Karab Longjong lived in a cave. The cave did not always protect him from the rain. He did not have a good pot, just a broken clay one. He had one yak hoof—that was his serving spoon. Also, his clothes were ragged and poor. That was Karab Longjong's style. The messengers also observed Milarepa and saw that he lived in a similar fashion.

After receiving the reports Godan Khan asked Sakya Pandita, "Why did you say that Karab Longjong is the richest person in Tibet and that Milarepa is the most successful? My messengers said they are so poor." Sakya Pandita replied, "Karab Longjong may appear to be poor, but he feels in his heart and mind that he has everything. He is absolutely happy and content. This is why he is the richest person in Tibet. And Milarepa? Milarepa has fulfilled his goal, and now he is fulfilling the goals of others. That is why he is the most successful person in Tibet."

Karab Longjong, Bagom, and other great masters insured that the Aro lineage maintained its vigor. Many people practiced the Aro teachings and achieved great realization. In the coming centuries, however, the terma tradition in Tibet became increasingly popular, even dominant. The Aro tradition gradually weakened and was eventually absorbed into various kama lineages. By the nineteenth century it was on the verge of dying out. Although in terms of content the Aro lineage is not that different from the rest of Dzogchen Semde or even from general Buddhism, Aro Yeshe Jungne and his teachings have a unique style and flavor. At the same time they are extremely powerful. Therefore, in order to revitalize and preserve this special lineage for future generations, the great master Patrul Rinpoche collected all the Aro teachings from the various kama lineages, edited them, and put them into a single text called *Clear Elucidation of True Nature: An Esoteric Instruction on the Sublime Approach of Ati*, or *Thegchok Ati Mennag Neluk Salton* in Tibetan. It is in large measure owing to the great kindness and industry of Patrul Rinpoche that the Aro lineage began to thrive again and has now come to the West.

Lineage is very important in Buddhism. It is of particular importance in Vajrayana Buddhism and in the Nyingma school. Lineage is not only the historical record and genealogy of masters who have held a particular teaching, nor is it only the teaching itself expressed verbally or on a page. These are important, of course, but what is even more important is the spiritual vitality of that teaching as it is transmitted from mind to mind and heart to heart. In other words, the lineage lives in the thoughts, words, and deeds of persons who have received, cherished, practiced, and accomplished it. Therefore, if you have a book of profound teachings, study and try to implement them. If you are not connected to a master who holds the lineage of that teaching, you will not get very far.

The Dzogchen lineage is called the "Stainless Golden Mountain Lineage," or the "Stainless Golden Chain Lineage." This lineage flows powerfully from the Buddha Samantabhadra; it flows eternally. The Buddha Samantabhadra is the true nature of your mind; it is the state of infinite love, compassion, wisdom, and power. The Dzogchen lineage has therefore always been with you—it *is* you—but you have not yet realized it. You now have the opportunity to realize this lineage and to become what you truly are. You do this by connecting to a master who has realized his or her mind to be the Buddha Samantabhadra, and by practicing as instructed by that master with devotion, courage, and commitment. This is how the teachings have been preserved, this is how they are transmitted, this is how they are practiced, and this is how enlightenment is attained.

# 2: The Inner Hermitage

As practitioners of the Buddha's teachings we should cultivate the three hermitage qualities. Of course, we are already in a hermitage, in this beautiful retreat center in the Catskill Mountains known as Padma Samye Ling. This is the outer hermitage, and it is very special and important. But we also need to activate the inner hermitage qualities of body, speech, and mind. When these three are activated and maintained, even if we cannot get to an outer hermitage our practice will be strong and effective.

Hermitage of the body means reducing mundane activities and emphasizing Dharma. We direct our minds to positive qualities such as love and compassion, joy and appreciation, and with these as a foundation perform meritorious activities. Avoiding actions that are harmful, doing what is beneficial for us and for others—this is known as the hermitage of the body.

Hermitage of the speech means trying to avoid all talk that is disrespectful, harsh, and negative—anything that brings harm to yourself and others. This kind of talk is known in the Buddha's teaching as gossip. Gossip has no good qualities. Once begun, gossip tends to travel, accumulate, and disturb many people. Reduce and ultimately avoid gossip—this is part of the practice of the hermitage of speech. Another aspect of the hermitage of speech is to not spend much time talking about trivial things. In other words, reduce mundane conversation. Then there is silence. When you practice silence you are self-contained and more inward-looking. You notice the busyness of your body, speech, and mind and your self-awareness grows. Eliminate gossip, reduce mundane conversation, and practice silence—all these make up what is known as the hermitage of speech.

The third one is hermitage of the mind. Reduce grasping, clinging, doubt, hesitation, and all thoughts related to the five poisons—ignorance, attachment, anger, arrogance, and jealousy. However these emotions manifest in you—individually, in combinations, or all together—stay away from them, do not indulge them, let them go. That is known as hermitage of the mind.

When you maintain the three inner hermitage qualities, you will experience the beautiful, serene environment of the outer hermitage even if you are in the city. In fact when the inner hermitage is strong and stable, you yourself become the outer hermitage, and beings, simply by being near you, will experience comfort and peace, just as if they traveled far away to a mountain retreat. Therefore, value these inner hermitage qualities, and nurture them as much as you can.

We further strengthen and glorify the hermitage qualities of body, speech, and mind by reading the Buddha's teachings, such as the sutras and tantras; by chanting mantras; by performing positive actions; and by always aspiring to do even better in our spiritual practice. This will increase our realization and decrease and ultimately uproot all negative thoughts and emotions. Cultivate devotion, love, compassion, kindness, respect, and appreciation, and practice the six paramitas—all these good thoughts and deeds are so important. This has been a brief description of how to establish, maintain, and increase the inner hermitage of body, speech, and mind.

# 3: Bodhichitta and Impermanence

WHENEVER WE ARE going to meditate on Dzogchen, we should always start with the foundation practices. According to the great Dzogchen master and teacher Garab Dorje, these foundation practices are cultivating bodhichitta and reflecting on impermanence.

We begin with bodhichitta. Bodhichitta is the foundation not only of Dzogchen but of all Dharma practice. Bodhichitta has two aspects: wishing or aspirational bodhichitta, and actualizing bodhichitta. Wishing bodhichitta does not mean only reciting the words of a bodhichitta prayer; it means to keep generating genuine care and concern for all beings from your heart. Continually cultivate the four boundless thoughts: boundless love, boundless compassion, boundless joy, and boundless equanimity. Pray that all beings will enjoy long life, health, prosperity, and the fulfillment of all their wishes that are in accord with Dharma. Pray that they attain complete enlightenment. At the same time, pray that your desire and ability to help all beings keeps growing. This is wishing bodhichitta. Actualizing bodhichitta means to help others according to your abilities and their needs—it is putting wishing bodhichitta into action in words and deeds.

Bodhichitta is the way of the great Dzogchen masters. For example, Patrul Rinpoche always contemplated and practiced the four boundless thoughts and spent his entire life helping others. When we read the life story of the great master Jigme Lingpa, we see numerous examples of the greatness of his love and compassion—the degree and strength of his bodhichitta was enormous. The biography of Jigme Lingpa tells that earlier in his life, when he was practicing in a hermitage, he was very poor, but whenever he saw suffering people, such as beggars, he gave them the clothes off his back. He did not have much to eat—maybe one bowl of soup—but would give whatever he had to the hungry. Patrul Rinpoche and Jigme Lingpa are role models and examples.

This is true also of the great Dzogchen master Longchenpa. And not only these three, but in fact all the great Dzogchen masters throughout history were also great practitioners of bodhichitta. They practiced the teachings they were given, realized those teachings, and shared the fruits of their realization with others. This was also the way of Buddha Shakyamuni. We are following in the footsteps of these great masters. This means we should cultivate and manifest bodhichitta in our hearts and minds, in our words, and in our actions. We should strive to increase, deepen, and expand our capacity to help others. This is the foundation of our Dzogchen practice.

Then, according to Garab Dorje's teaching, after cultivating bodhichitta we should reflect on impermanence. It is very important to think about impermanence, because each moment, every experience, and life itself is impermanent. When we think of impermanence we are thinking of time. Time is fleeting; each moment passes and we have less and less time. This means that time is precious. And time is ripe with opportunities. For example, at this time we have gathered together to discuss the teachings of Aro Yeshe Jungne. We can share our knowledge, explore and deepen our experience of the true nature, and we can grow. This time of our gathering is not accidental, coincidental, or casual—it is wondrous and profound. Many beautiful ingredients have come together to make this gathering possible. We have every reason to feel gratitude and joy. We are in this beautiful place, studying these beautiful teachings, we ourselves are beautiful—what is missing? Therefore we should cultivate courage and commitment and use this time and all time wisely, to bring good things to ourselves and others, now and in the future.

The Dudjom Tersar Ngöndro says, "Everything born is impermanent and bound to die." And it is true; everything passes. But reflecting on impermanence does not have to be sad. It can inspire us to fully appreciate and embrace this unique, one-of-a-kind moment. The past has passed and the future has not yet begun. We are here. The teachings say that reflection on impermanence can bring us back to the true nature where we belong. This means that our enlightenment can occur right now.

# 4: Opening the Aro Text

WITH BODHICHITTA and impermanence as our beautiful foundation, we go to the text itself. As we said, in the nineteenth century the great master Patrul Rinpoche collected and edited all of Aro Yeshe Jungne's teachings, then published them in a single volume entitled *Clear Elucidation of True Nature*. This is the text we will be exploring.

PATRUL RINPOCHE

Patrul Rinpoche begins with the words, "I pay homage to the glorious and supreme lamas." This includes Buddha Samantabhadra, Buddha Shakyamuni, Guru Padmasambhava, and all the great Dzogchen masters of the past. Patrul Rinpoche did not create this teaching by himself, nor was it created by Aro Yeshe Jungne. This is a continuous lineage teaching, the words of primordial wisdom revealed and shared by many great beings. This is the reason Patrul Rinpoche begins by paying homage to the masters of this lineage. In particular, though not explicitly, he honors his own root teacher, Jigme Gyalwai Nyugu.

After the homage Patrul Rinpoche says that the infinite sentient beings of this world have different levels or degrees of capability to understand, practice, and actualize the Dzogchen teachings. Some have high capability, some have medium capability, and some have lesser capability. The great master goes on to say that even though differences in capability exist, everyone has the potential and deserves the opportunity to attain enlightenment. For that reason he will share Aro's simple instructions on how to meditate on and actualize Dzogchen.

# 5: What Is the Nature of Your Mind?

When you meditate on Dzogchen you should first search and discover the nature of your mind. Your mind is vast. The limitless universe and all that is within it appears within your mind. All manner of suffering and joy takes place within your mind. Countless thoughts come and go effortlessly through your mind. The teachings say that everything is mind. Now the time has come at last to realize whether this is true or not. You must do the work. No one else can do it for you. You are exploring the nature of your own mind. It is you who must resolve this matter—do not leave it in a hazy, vague state. It is not enough to say, "I heard it, it sounds good, I presume it is right." In order to do Dzogchen meditation properly you cannot simply agree with what others have said about the nature of the mind; you must look again and again into your own mind and come to a decisive understanding as to its nature.

This is known as the way of contemplation. Through contemplation you will reach a conclusion, and have the final say. You have heard what the Buddha, the lineage masters, and your root teacher have taught about the nature of the mind, and you have read about it in books. All of this is generally good, of course, but now you have to determine for yourself whether or not what the teachers and the texts say is true. You are making the quality check once and for all. For that reason Patrul Rinpoche here uses the expression *dal sha chu*. This is Tibetan for "you must make the final proof." This means that the time to know is now.

You can begin by seeking the location of your mind. Many people believe mind is located inside the body, in the brain or in the heart. In particular, most people in modern times think the mind is in the brain. Now, look within your brain and search for your mind. Can you find it? Is it in the heart? Search for it there. Perhaps your mind is in your brain and heart simultaneously. Seek your mind in both places simultaneously. When you search for your mind in your brain, heart, or in both places at once, do you find a solidly existing mind anywhere?

Mind, according to Buddhism, is not matter. Brain and heart are matter. The source of matter, depending on which system and terminology we use, is thought to be atoms and molecules or the four elements—earth, water, fire, and wind. Atoms, molecules, and the four elements are tangible; mind is not tangible. That which is tangible can be resisted or blocked; mind cannot be resisted or blocked. Matter is conditioned; mind is unconditioned. Matter is subject to many laws; mind is subject to none. You should determine for yourself whether or not this is so. You should explore within the laboratory of your own mind the differences between mind and matter. The fact is that they are completely different. This is the resolution that the Buddha and all the great masters made, and this can be your understanding too.

Matter can be measured, quantified, and qualified until the absolute levels are reached. Measurement, quantification, and qualification apply to matter alone. Mind is beyond this; it is in a totally different category. This is not something you have to believe; it is, however, something very worthwhile that you can discover. Inquire whether or not the mind can be measured, quantified, and qualified. How many miles is the mind? How tall, how wide? What shape, what thickness? What does the mind weigh? Ask these questions and you will quickly realize they are appropriate only to objects of the tangible world and absolutely inapplicable to mind. Mind has nothing to do with miles, height, width, or shape. Mind—your own mind—is boundless. If you look within, you will see.

In addition to be being boundless, your own mind is unconditional love. This is not tradition or dogma or belief. The Buddha did not decide that mind is boundless and unconditional love on a whim and make it into a rule. Buddha discovered what was there within his own mind, and realized that what was true within his own mind was also true within the minds of all others. The Buddha also said we should examine his words the way a goldsmith examines gold. He never said that we must blindly believe him. He said that we should investigate the matter for ourselves. The Buddha is talking about nature, and nature is an open door. We can and should open nature's door, look for ourselves, and discover the truth. We should not follow blindly or willfully what someone else said just because they are famous. The fact is that the truth is not something Buddha made up; it is not something that belongs to him alone. What is truth is available to everyone.

You should continue your investigation of mind. Does your mind have a color? Is it yellow, orange, red, blue, or green? Is your mind composed of atoms and molecules? Is it composed of the four elements? Is your mind hot or icy cold? Investigate further—does time apply to your mind? In other words, does your mind belong to the past, present, and future? Look at this; be thorough. See for yourself that color, composition, temperature, and time do not apply to mind. This is how you should examine your mind. This is how you bring this inquiry to conclusion. By constant, vigilant inquiry you will come to recognize and confirm that mind is boundless, beyond any and all categories. When you know for sure that your own mind is boundless, there is no need to ask any more questions. Now it is time to meditate, which means simply to relax into this boundlessness.

Boundless mind is always with you, wherever you are. The teachings say that once you have performed this detailed inquiry and have attained a good understanding of the nature of your mind, from that point on your practice should be more direct. It is no longer necessary to ask many questions. Just look at your own mind and ask, "Who is analyzing the nature of the mind?" The moment you do this both the analyzer and the analysis merge into boundlessness. You can also look within and inquire, "Where is my mind?" The moment you ask that question and seek an answer you behold the boundless state. Another question you can ask is, "Who am I?"

Any and all of the questions you pose to your mind regarding its nature do not yield answers. There are no answers. The questions themselves dissolve. There is nothing to seek and find, nothing to grasp, there is nothing solid at all. Everything opens to the boundless state. This is the true nature; in Buddhism it is called "emptiness." In describing the state of emptiness, the Buddha used the words *inexpressible* and *inconceivable*. The inexpressible, inconceivable state of emptiness that is the nature of the mind is the essence of the Buddha's vast Prajnaparamita teachings. And it is the heart of his Dzogchen teaching as well.

After you discover the true nature by inquiry, then simply abide, with confidence, in that state. According to the Aro teachings as well as the teachings of other great masters elsewhere, you should meditate on that state as long as you can without being disturbed by thoughts. Meditation here means to maintain and grow increasingly familiar with your boundless, inexpressible mind. Of course, even when you recognize the nature of your mind, habitual patterns of thought will return and this state of recognition will be lost. That is why the teachings mention that in the beginning the glimpse of realization comes but doesn't stay long. It is like opening a door on a windy day. The door stays open for a moment, then the wind slams it shut. How long the door of recognizing the true nature remains open varies from person to person. Some people can remain in the true nature all the time, some for a while, and others only briefly. But everyone has the potential to achieve permanent recognition.

Directly experiencing the true nature of your own mind is known as self-awareness, self-recognition, or self-realization. What you have acquired by investigation and analysis must now be maintained in meditation with courage, commitment, and confidence. Again, relax into your own boundlessness. Now you no longer have to analyze, investigate, or inquire into the nature of your mind. When you know and are abiding in the nature of your mind—that is to say, when you are meditating—analysis, investigation, and inquiry are fabrications.

You have recognized the nature of your mind, and you are abiding in the open, thought-free state. Suddenly thoughts return: pleasant thoughts and unpleasant thoughts. Who determines, this thought is pleasant and that thought is unpleasant? Who judges, this is good and that is bad? This is dirty and that is clean? This is high and that is low? This is spiritual and that is worldly? No one outside you makes these judgments. Your own mind does. The next time a thought arises, do not judge it; simply look directly to your mind itself. When you do this, the thought immediately dissolves. This happens because all thoughts are baseless, speechless, inexpressible, and inconceivable. Mind is empty and what arises from mind is also empty.

# 6: Duality: Mind Deceiving Mind

Your mind does not solidly exist, yet it is active, producing thought after thought without effort. Mind is empty and what arises from mind is empty. This means thought is empty too. But when this is not recognized, when you believe your thoughts are real and true, it is known as duality. When you are experiencing duality it is inevitable that you will speak and act on behalf of your thoughts. Dualistic thoughts, words, and deeds pile up; all kinds of divisions and boundaries, such as "self" and "other," "mine" and "yours," are created and defended. Mind becomes turbulent and negative emotions erupt—many uncomfortable and even painful things internally and externally can occur. The teachings call these "nightmare visions." These nightmare visions are the result of waves upon waves of fabrication and deceit connected to ego, or "I." All of this emanates from emptiness mind; not a single component of this has a basis in reality. However, when emptiness mind is not understood, the nightmare visions seem real and are experienced in very real ways. Thus it is called a "magical display."

When your mind creates negativity and you project this onto the external environment, it will affect the external environment adversely and will bounce back to you. The negativity that you receive from the external environment inspires more negativity within you. More negativity is projected out again, and more comes bouncing back. You always bear the consequences of the deceptions of your dualistic mind.

If you truly want to put an end to duality and its deceptions once and for all, it is necessary to discover the nature of your mind. Look into your mind and reach a final conclusion. For this reason, in ancient times Dzogchen masters said to their students, "Go out, find your mind, and bring it back to me." The masters sent their students out into the world or the wilderness for a few days or weeks, or even for as long as a month, to search for their minds. Then, once they discovered their minds, the students would return to their masters and tell them what they found. This practice works in ways similar to a Zen koan. Therefore look at your own mind—search out and discover its nature. Come to a resolution. This is what you need to do in order to put duality to rest for good.

# 7: The Nine Levels of Capability

THE ARO TEACHINGS divide Dzogchen practitioners into three categories: (1) high capability practitioners, (2) medium capability practitioners, and (3) lesser capability practitioners.

High capability practitioners realize the Dzogchen teachings immediately. Medium capability practitioners do so gradually. Lesser capability practitioners require more time and effort. Even within the three categories there can be differing levels of capacity. For this reason the Aro teachings subdivide each one of these categories into three, so that there are nine in all:

1. high capability practitioners of the highest caliber
2. high capability practitioners of medium caliber
3. high capability practitioners of lesser caliber
4. medium capability practitioners of the highest caliber
5. medium capability practitioners of medium caliber
6. medium capability practitioners of lesser caliber
7. lesser capability practitioners of the highest caliber
8. lesser capability practitioners of medium caliber
9. lesser capability practitioners of lesser caliber

We will now explore the instructions given for each one of these nine levels, beginning with the first.

# 8: Instructions for High Capability Practitioners of the Highest Caliber

Once you have a good realization of the nature of your mind—once you know for certain that the nature of your mind is boundless and inexpressible—how will you maintain it? If you are a high capability practitioner of the highest caliber, you know that whether the mind is abiding in the natural state or whether the mind is moving, it is no other than mind. You know that when mind is abiding it is empty, and when it is moving it is empty. This means that you know that when the mind moves—that is, when thoughts arise—it does not affect the nature of the mind.

When you are abiding in the nature of mind many different thoughts arise. Thoughts arise because your mind, in addition to being boundless and inexpressible, is full of power and energy, and that power and energy create, display, and dissolve thoughts unceasingly. Your mind is active and busy—this is part of its nature. But even though thoughts keep arising, nothing changes regarding the nature of your mind. The nature of your mind is empty, and the nature of thought is empty too. If you look into the heart of any thought that arises, that thought will dissolve on the spot. Even if you don't do anything at all, the thought will still dissolve. That is why the great master Guru Padmasambhava said that thoughts move through the mind like wind moves through the sky. The wind moves through the sky in different directions and at different speeds, stopping and starting, always unpredictable. The wind cannot be separated from the sky, and the sky remains unaffected by the wind. Therefore the high capability practitioner of the highest caliber experiences no difference between abiding and movement. When the mind moves it is fine, and when the mind is still it is fine. There are no categories and no choices to be made within and for the minds of such practitioners.

Observe this for yourself. When you are meditating, how long can your mind abide? Then, when your mind moves, does that movement disturb you or not? When your mind moves and you are not disturbed, this means you are a high capability practitioner of the highest caliber. In other words, when you do not experience the slightest difference between stillness and thought—when it is all the same for you—you are at the peak of the Dzogchen mountain. At that time you can practice in the busiest, most chaotic places—for instance, in Times Square in New York City or in the railway stations in India. The Dzogchen teachings say that when your realization is strong, being in such turbulent places is not disruptive at all; rather, it serves to enhance and deepen your practice.

When this is your experience, you are in the wisdom state. All your perceptions are wisdom perceptions. All your conceptions are wisdom conceptions. All your thoughts are wisdom's display. You have the same realization as Buddha Shakyamuni, Guru Padmasambhava, and all the great masters, such as Garab Dorje, Shri Singha, and Longchenpa. The great masters do not make distinctions. Their realization is profound and unshakable. For them everything is the display of the true nature.

Thoughts and emotions may arise for a time due to habitual patterns, but for these practitioners all such mental events are instantly liberated into the natural state. Emotions and thoughts, however strong, cannot bind them because they instantly merge into the great emptiness state. By way of example, the teachings say that if you are being tied by ropes, the ropes catch fire and burn to ashes. It is impossible to be bound.

Thoughts and emotions may come, but they are expressions or reflections of emptiness. This is the teaching of the Prajnaparamita, Madhyamaka, Mahamudra, and Dzogchen. Therefore great Dzogchen practitioners do not accept and reject. There is nothing to figure out and nothing to choose—everything is the display and expression of the natural state. At this point in the text, master Patrul Rinpoche quotes Orgyen Rinpoche, "The Precious One from Orgyen," which is one of Guru Padmasambhava's names, who said, "The nature of thought is dharmakaya." *Dharmakaya* is a synonym for emptiness. Guru Padmasambhava is saying there is no difference between thought and emptiness—thought is emptiness.

The great masters who have this realization transcend all limitations; their minds are utterly open and free, which is why they can effortlessly perform miracles. Owing to their great compassion they will say and do anything at all that will inspire us to seek and find the freedom that they embody. These miraculous words and deeds are known as manifestations of "crazy wisdom." These manifestations are crazy from our perspective. How can a human being fly unaided through the sky? How can someone walk on water, appear in several places at once, or live for thousands of years? Our regimented minds say, "impossible." To these great masters, however, nothing is impossible.

# 9: How Practitioners of All Levels Should Practice the Aro Teachings

When we put the Aro teachings into practice, we begin by generating bodhichitta—the thought of love and compassion for all sentient beings—and then cultivate the four boundless thoughts. Next, we meditate on impermanence, reflecting on the fleeting nature, as well as the preciousness, of the world and of ourselves. We are beautiful beings and are intimately connected to these sublime teachings. We have the opportunity right here and now to open our minds to encompass and embody the infinite universe. We have the opportunity to help and inspire others to do the same. This is a cause for joy, appreciation, devotion, and celebration. With the desire to benefit all beings firmly in our hearts, with the realization that now is the time to put the precious teachings into practice, and with courage and commitment to persevere in this, there is no doubt that we will accomplish something meaningful for ourselves and others. Then, when it is time to leave this world, we will do so with joy and fulfillment. With these thoughts, feel the presence of Guru Padmasambhava, the Buddha, and all the Dzogchen lineage masters vividly and strongly. Pray for their blessings that we can fulfill their intentions as well as our own. These are the foundation practices.

Next, introduce—or reintroduce—the nature of your mind. Ask the question, "Where is my mind?" When you ask this question, you do not receive an answer. All the great masters say that no answer *is* the answer; that the speechless state is enlightenment. Now that you have arrived at the answerless state, which is enlightenment itself, simply relax. This is known as the emptiness of mind. The mind is emptiness, so rest in its emptiness. While you are experiencing the emptiness of mind do not create or harbor conceptions about the mind being empty. That is a fabrication—do not fabricate. Simply be in the moment. When thoughts come, do not reject or follow them. Thoughts appear and disappear on their own—nothing should be done about them. Use mindfulness as a support for your practice. Maintain the natural state in this way for ten, fifteen, or twenty minutes. While you are practicing emptiness meditation, occasionally bring up joy, appreciation, and devotion as well as love and compassion for a few moments—then return to emptiness. This will bring more vitality to your emptiness meditation.

At the end of your session, once again generate bodhichitta, wishing good things for all sentient beings. Remember, at the present time the true nature is not realized by everyone. Pray that everyone will attain this wisdom, that they will understand the true nature exactly as it is, so that violence and suffering as well as their causes will be uprooted. The good wishes that should conclude every practice session are known as dedication prayers.

During the postmeditation period, apply the three hermitage qualities of body, speech, and mind. This is a brief summary of how to practice the teachings of the masters Aro Yeshe Jungne and Patrul Rinpoche for people of all levels. Do you have any questions?

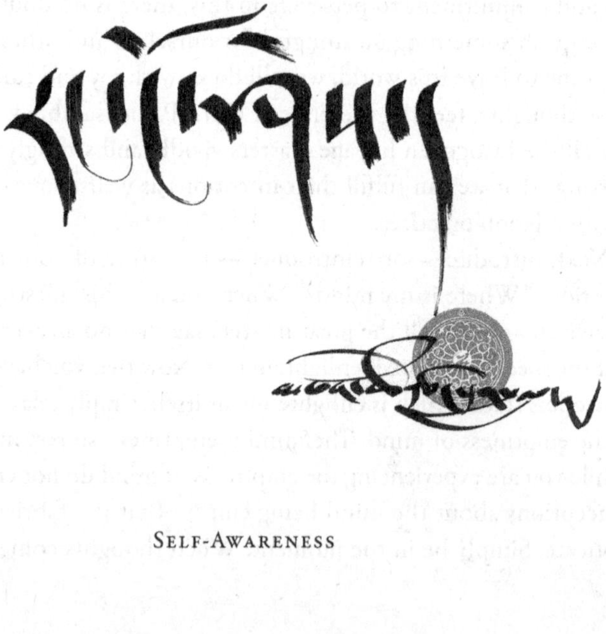

SELF-AWARENESS

## Questions and Answers

*Is everything mind?*

Yes, everything is mind. The five sensory experiences, all thoughts and emotions, the entirety of our physical and mental world—it is all mind.

At this time we are not investigating where physical objects come from, but rather we are looking at the perception of those objects, how we experience them, and also at thoughts and emotions. We are taking the close and quick approach in order to discover the true nature of all experience. The true nature of all experience is mind. This is not something you are obliged to believe; it is something to find out for yourself. Look into the matter, and as long as you have doubt, keep looking. If you want to increase your stability in Dzogchen meditation, developing certain knowledge and clear recognition that everything is mind is very important, so by all means keep up this inquiring practice until you are certain. Once you are certain that everything is mind, the Dzogchen teachings say that you should ask, "Where is my mind now?" At that moment look directly at your mind. When you look at your mind and do not find any location at all, you have arrived at the true nature. Then you abide in the true nature state you just discovered. Sometimes in the Dzogchen teachings this is called "meditating on the state with no conceptions." It is also called "no mind."

*Doesn't it say in the Prajnaparamita and Zen teachings that if we realize emptiness there is no need to meditate or practice?*

That's true. If we have that realization, the purpose of meditation has been fulfilled. If we have a perfect understanding of emptiness, we are free from duality. If we are free from duality, we do not need to practice.

But if we do not have this level of realization and follow the teachings that say meditation and practice are unnecessary, we are fooling ourselves. We are misinterpreting the Buddha's teachings and are going in the wrong direction. We will fall back into samsara.

*The general Buddhist teachings say that body, speech, and mind should always be engaged in meritorious activities; that we must train ourselves in virtue. But in Zen they compare this to cleaning ourselves with dirty water. How do you compare this Zen teaching to the Dzogchen teaching?*

When you have realization of the absolute truth—when you have perfect Zen or Dzogchen realization—you do not need to practice; you are already and always in the perfect practice state. Otherwise, to simply say, "I don't need to practice," is a manifestation of dualistic thinking. What is the purpose of practice? The purpose of practice is to purify duality. When you are realized, practice and nonpractice are dualistic conceptions, and you are beyond those conceptions. Until that time, the teachings always say to put wisdom and skillful means together. If you do not have realization, you cannot follow the absolute truth alone and reject the teachings on the relative truth. It is said that if you are always looking at the sky and never watch the ground, you can fall and break your collarbone, and it is true. The Buddha gave many teachings on the relative truth, such as the Vinaya and the Bodhisattvayana. If all beings had perfect realization, the Buddha would not have had to give those teachings. People who have the highest realization, like Zen and Dzogchen masters, are always in the practicing state. From the dualistic perspective we can say they no longer need to practice. But they achieved their goal, just as the Buddha did. Buddha Shakyamuni fulfilled his mission. Whether he sat on a cushion, walked in the city, or was engaged in conversation, whatever he was doing, he was always in the natural state. Notions of practice and nonpractice—he went beyond that. All those great practitioners accomplished this same realization.

The teachings say to merge samsara and nirvana into a single state. They do not say that we should reject one and accept the other. Rejection and acceptance are duality games. That is what we have always been doing, which is why we are deluded. If we want to get out of duality we have to cooperate with the teachings. Until realization, you must cultivate good conduct; once you are realized you do not have to make efforts toward good conduct. When you are realized you are always in the state of good conduct.

*Is it possible that we might cling to emptiness?*

The Buddha gave teachings on emptiness so that we will give up clinging to phenomena. He also said that emptiness is empty. The Buddha said this so we would stop clinging to emptiness. We should not cling to phenomena or to emptiness—the goal is to be free of all clinging.

*How would you compare the Buddhist and scientific views regarding the location of the mind, as well as the mind's relationship to matter?*

For the scientific view you will have to go to a scientist's laboratory. But according to the Buddhist point of view, mind and matter are completely different. For instance, mind, unlike matter, can travel instantaneously. Your body may be here in New York, but in a moment your mind can travel to California, or to the other side of the world. Wherever mind wants to go, it can go. And mind can communicate very easily with other minds. This is all possible from the perspective of duality.

Nondualistic mind can do infinitely more. Nondualistic mind, also known as "wisdom mind," is much deeper and more subtle than dualistic mind. For example, nondualistic mind is beyond time. It can travel from this present life to the next one. It can travel from a past life to this present one. It can witness countless aeons in a single moment.

Regarding the location of the mind, many Buddhist teachings say its headquarters is in the heart and its activity center is in the brain. In this way, the heart is like the White House and the brain is like the Capitol or the Pentagon. Or the heart is the powerhouse of the mind, and the brain is its electricity.

Some people think the mind is the brain. If mind is the brain, then when a person dies and the brain is intact, why does the mind not function? What exactly is death from the perspective of mind? Scientists consider and explore these matters using their own tools and techniques. We are doing so according to the Dzogchen teaching.

*How do we avoid clinging to emptiness?*

The Buddha used analogies like dreams, magic, mirages, reflections of the moon in water, illusions, and echoes to point out the nature of emptiness so that we don't cling to it. He also said that emptiness is like the sky and space. Is it possible to hold on to the sky?

*It seems like there are many names for mind, such as "consciousness." Is consciousness the same as mind?*

In Tibetan and Sanskrit, there are also many names for mind. And yes, consciousness and mind are the same.

*How does consciousness function in relation to the notion of "I" according to the Buddhist perspective?*

In the Abhidharma there are extensive teachings on this topic. The Abhidharma explores the meaning of "I." It asks, "What is this 'I'? Is it consciousness? Are 'I' and consciousness one and the same?" The Abhidharma goes on to say that "I" is not consciousness; it is one of the doors, or windows, of consciousness. "I" is present only when consciousness manifests it. It is similar to objects in the physical world: you see these objects only when you focus on them. If your consciousness is focused on something else, you will not see them. Similarly, "I" goes in and out of consciousness.

*Can you say more about the mind being in the heart?*

In Buddhism it is said that the mind resides primarily in the heart. This means the heart is extremely important. When your heart stops, you pass away. The mind stops functioning at that moment.

*What is the difference between the mind and the nature of the mind?*

It depends on the teaching. In the Sutrayana teachings—that is, in the Mind Only and Madhyamaka schools—the mind and the nature of the mind are the same. But in Dzogchen they are different.

In Dzogchen what we call "mind" is dualistic mind, the mind trapped in thoughts and emotions. The "nature of the mind" is the mind when it is free from thoughts and emotions. There are many teachings in Dzogchen related to how we distinguish and separate the mind from the nature of the mind, and how, once they are distinguished, to abide in the nature.

The Dzogchen teachings have other names for dualistic mind and its nature. For example, conceptual mind is also known as *alaya*, and the mind free of concepts is often called dharmakaya. Then there is *sem* and *semnyi*. *Sem* is dualistic mind, and *semnyi* is the nature of mind. There is a Dzogchen teaching by Longchenpa called *Semnyi Ngalso* in Tibetan, which literally translates into English as *Relaxing in the Nature of Mind*. A synonym used in Dzogchen for the nature of mind is *semche dorje*, which means "original mind." And then of course there is *marigpa* and *rigpa*, which refer respectively to impure, twisted awareness and pure awareness.

*I heard that it is important when practicing vipashyana to keep the eyes absolutely still. Is this also important for Dzogchen practice?*

There are two principal practices in Dzogchen: trekchö and tögal. The teachings for trekchö practice say you should keep your eyes open and gaze into space. When you open your eyes and gaze into space during trekchö practice, it is perfectly fine to blink and also to swallow. Feel comfortable and relaxed when you practice trekchö. For tögal practice, however, you should definitely avoid moving your eyes.

# 10: A Dzogchen Overview

Sentient beings have diverse capacities for understanding the true nature. This is why the Buddha gave so many different teachings. These teachings are like a vast banquet with all kinds of delicious dishes suitable to every taste.

The Buddha's teachings can be grouped into three levels. The foundation level is the Hinayana, the second level is the Mahayana, and the third and highest level is the Vajrayana. All of the Hinayana teachings are contained in the Mahayana, and all of the Hinayana and Mahayana teachings are contained in the Vajrayana. This means the Vajrayana is the complete teaching of the Buddha.

The masters of the Nyingma school of Tibetan Buddhism divided the Hinayana, Mahayana, and Vajrayana into nine levels, or *yanas*. *Yana* can be translated into English as "vehicle" or "carrier." In the same way we just discussed, the first yana is contained in the second, the first and second yanas are contained in the third, and so on, until we reach the ninth and ultimate yana: Dzogchen. Dzogchen means "Great Completion" or "Great Perfection," because it alone contains all the previous eight yanas, as well as itself. This means that Dzogchen is the all-encompassing, whole, complete teaching of the Buddha.

Over the centuries many people who practiced Dzogchen reached the highest levels of realization. While many people have attained the highest realization by practicing the teachings of other Buddhist schools, even more have done so within the Nyingma lineage through the practice of Dzogchen. Why is this? It is because Dzogchen is so clear, direct, and powerful. It is well known that many Dzogchen practitioners achieved the transcendental wisdom rainbow body. Other Dzogchen practitioners who did not achieve the rainbow body, and who were not known to later generations by titles like "great lama," or "mahasiddha," still achieved complete realization of the true nature. In humble, simple, quiet ways, these practitioners reached the ultimate goal of life.

In general, when we practice Dzogchen we accumulate and accomplish the two merits of skillful means and wisdom in union. If we separate skillful means and wisdom, and choose one and reject the other, our practice is not all-encompassing and complete and is therefore no longer Dzogchen. In particular, this Aro teaching is based more on wisdom. In other words, it focuses on view and meditation. It is grounded more on the absolute level since it is a direct teaching on the true nature. Even so, if we want to actualize this teaching we still must practice it through the union of skillful means and wisdom.

Dzogchen is the highest teaching, and Dzogchen practitioners are of the highest capacity. The first of the Aro teachings, which we have already touched upon, are for high capability practitioners of the highest caliber. For these people the universe and their own minds are inseparable in the enlightened state. They experience all phenomena as pure, and do not create divisions such as "subject" and "object." They abide in nonduality. With regard to their understanding, there is nothing to add and nothing to subtract, nothing to gain and nothing to lose—everything is in the Great Completion, Great Perfection state. Whether their minds are abiding or moving, nothing changes. Quiet and peaceful mind, active mind—it is all the same. Nor do they distinguish between meditation and postmeditation. Whatever comes, moves, changes, and goes is the manifestation of the natural state, spacious and free. These practitioners are beyond hope and fear of both samsara and nirvana. The teaching here says, "Originally enlightened—both appearance and mind itself." Truly, for these practitioners everything is fulfilled. For the rest of us, this level of fulfillment is close at hand, even imminent, as long as we keep practicing.

# 11: Instructions for High Capability Practitioners of Medium Caliber

This next teaching is for high capability practitioners of medium caliber. After completing the foundation practices, these people should reintroduce the nature of their minds by asking, "Where is my mind?" or, "Who is meditating?" When you ask yourself one of these questions, there is no longer any subject or object. Subject and object are conceptions. These questions immediately dissolve conceptions. You reach the answerless state; everything is open. Now you meditate on that state, abiding naturally, without changing a thing. Do not add conceptions. We sentient beings are deluded because we have added so many conceptions to our original nature. By adding conceptions, and holding on to and analyzing those conceptions, delusion grows thicker and thicker. The moment you reach the answerless state all those conceptions vanish and delusion is gone. You have reached the natural state. You should rest right there.

Resting in the natural state also means that you should not intentionally focus on anything. Focusing is duality—when you focus you are re-creating subject and object. Do not deliberately provoke thoughts of any kind. At the same time, when different thoughts arise by themselves, do not be distracted. Use mindfulness as a support, and let them go. So the key to keeping up this profound practice is to remain in the natural state without focus and without distraction. For this reason the great Dzogchen master Guru Zhiwa said, "I never meditated, but I never missed the point."

When appearances come—that is, when perceptions or conceptions arise—they are meditation's display. Do not cling to them, but rather let them be what they are: natural, fleeting movements of the mind's great energy. Guru Zhiwa also said, "I never found anything that needed to be structured by conceptions." When we are stable in this state we will have no need to name, categorize, accept, or reject phenomena. Free of these and all such fabrications, we simply abide in the original, natural state. There is nothing else to meditate on.

Again, before we begin this meditation, in order to ignite it, generate bodhichitta and reflect on impermanence. We should also consider the special circumstances that connect us to this lineage teaching. We are among the luckiest people on earth—not everyone has the opportunity, inclination, and capacity to practice Dzogchen. We have every reason to feel joy, appreciation, and gratitude. With these beautiful thoughts, invoke and receive the lineage blessings with devotion. Generating bodhichitta, reflecting on impermanence, and expressing gratitude and devotion are expressions of enlightened mind. They are the relative manifestations of the absolute. Relative truth and absolute truth are a perfect unity. To accept one and reject the other is like accepting one of our eyes and rejecting the other. Also, it is incorrect to consider these foundation practices as a mere prelude to real meditation. To highlight and cultivate these qualities with good concentration is actually excellent meditation practice and will sharpen the clarity aspect of your mind. So begin with these foundation practices, do them well, and then, as the great master Aro taught and as we just discussed, identify and abide in the natural state with no distractions and no focus for as long as you can. Following that, with great inspiration and bodhichitta, dedicate the merit for all living beings. This is the complete practice that encompasses all aspects of the true nature.

Here the Aro teachings state that depending on your capabilities, if you practice continuously in this way for one week, two weeks, or for one month at the most, you will definitely get good realization. From then on you will be able to maintain the natural Dzogchen state without much effort. According to the Dzogchen tradition, this practice is called "Originally Liberated into Vast Space." The Mahamudra tradition calls it the "Self-Illuminating Technique."

# 12: Instructions for High Capability Practitioners of Lesser Caliber

Since Dzogchen is the highest teaching of the Buddha, everyone who practices Dzogchen is a high capability practitioner. Yet there are some slight differences in the ways we accept and assimilate the teachings, and also in the ways we manifest the result, so the instructions are adjusted accordingly. But in reality, there is no great variance in the capacities of people within the three or nine levels. We should understand the terms "high capability," "medium capability," and "lesser capability" as referring to readiness, or ripeness. These three levels of capability can also be understood as referring to different ranges of experience, from very experienced, to somewhat experienced, to just beginning.

The instructions for high capability practitioners of lesser caliber are as follows: continue abiding in the natural state of mind. In this respect the practice is the same as it is for people of the two highest levels. However, unlike persons of the highest two levels, high capability practitioners of lesser caliber continue to experience thoughts and emotions in the same ways ordinary people do. But unlike ordinary people, these practitioners do not grasp thoughts and emotions for long periods. Rather, these practitioners quickly bring themselves back to the nongrasping, open, and clear state of mind. They let go of thoughts and emotions, and swiftly return to the state of meditation, or the state of abiding, without being disturbed by additional fabrications. At that moment, the object of meditation is gone, and so is the subject.

These practitioners are also able to bring this realization into the postmeditation period. In this way there is no longer any difference between meditation and postmeditation for them. At all times and places, whenever thoughts and emotions arise, they catch them quickly with their mindfulness radar and free them without any trace of duality or clinging. They have become very skilled at liberating everything into the dharmakaya. So even though these practitioners continue to experience thoughts and emotions like ordinary beings, the way they handle these thoughts and emotions is completely different.

As we said, the teachings of Aro Yeshe Jungne belong primarily to the Mind Section of Dzogchen. In the terminology of the Mind Section, the particular instructions that are given for high capability practitioners of lesser caliber are known as "Without Thought, but Seeing Everything Brilliantly," or "Without Thought, but Seeing Everything Clearly, As It Is, with Omniscience." Here Patrul Rinpoche quotes the great Indian master Mitra Dzokyi, who visited Tibet around the twelfth century: "If you abide in the absolute state when appearances arise, you are accomplishing natural, spontaneous, and effortless meditation." That means you should keep abiding in the natural state even when perceptions and conceptions arise. Do not create identifications and categories. Do not divide or choose. Have no hope or fear regarding what arises; just leave everything as it is. If you keep this up in your meditation, you will progress naturally and effortlessly, and every spiritual accomplishment will spontaneously come.

These are the profound essence instructions of the Aro lineage. Keep them in your heart and mind. While doing formal meditation, and also during the postmeditation period, practice these teachings without doubt or hesitation. As you grow stronger in your capacity to abide in the natural state, your relationship and interaction with the universe will transform. You will no longer experience the universe as being external or separate from yourself. Instead, you will experience it manifesting itself to you through your six sense consciousnesses in the form of the six sense objects:

1. The object of eye consciousness is form, or body.
2. The object of ear consciousness is sound.
3. The object of tongue consciousness is taste.
4. The object of nose consciousness is smell.
5. The object of body consciousness is touch, or sensation.
6. The object of mind consciousness is thought, imagination, or thinking about the past, present, and future.

In the Dzogchen teachings it says, "Form is liberated, sound is liberated, taste is liberated, smell is liberated, touch is liberated, and imagination is liberated." This means that when you discover that the nature of your mind is perfect, you also discover that the nature of the six sensory experiences is perfect—thus the entire universe is perfect. Now everything you perceive is fluid, translucent, and beautiful. Grasping and clinging are gone. There is no more good and bad, high and low. There is no more hope and fear. You no longer believe that enlightenment is something to be attained in the future or that the pure land exists in a faraway place. Everything is already enlightened and the pure land is wherever you are.

Originally Liberated into Vast Space

People who have achieved the liberation of the six senses abide in the state of great blissfulness. We can read about the great yogis and yoginis of the past who lived in solitude in mountain caves with virtually nothing. From the dualistic perspective it may seem that these practitioners must have been lonely and miserable, but in actuality they were absolutely happy and content. We can also read about great masters and mahasiddhas who happened to be quite wealthy and powerful, but this did not make them haughty and proud. Circumstances and status, riches and poverty, what the dualistic mind deems good or bad, high or low, does not change the minds and hearts of realized beings. When we look at their faces they are always smiling, always joyful. At this point in the text, Patrul Rinpoche quotes from another Dzogchen teaching, "When the objects of the five senses appear, if you do not delude yourself by clinging, the realization of the Buddha is in your heart." In other words, nongrasping is buddhahood. For this reason, the great master Tilopa gave this final teaching to his foremost disciple, Naropa: "Son, appearances do not bind you; clinging binds you. Therefore, cut your clinging." And in the same way, the great master Pa Dampa Sangye, as well as his student, the wisdom dakini Machik Labdron, said, "If you recognize the mistakes of grasping and are able to abide in the natural state, then whatever thoughts come are themselves the meditation." This means that even when the most powerful negative emotions rise up within your mind, if you do not cling to them, they are wisdom.

In a single voice, all the great Dzogchen masters say to abide in the view, and when thoughts arise, to not follow or reject them. Let thoughts come, let thoughts go, and do not change, structure, or establish anything. Thoughts do not require any actions on your part. Thoughts are emptiness-appearance: transparent, unimpeded, and fresh. Good and bad, hope and fear, accepting and rejecting are the creations of dualistic mind. They are conceptions and delusions. The true nature of the mind is beyond conception and without delusion. It is called the absolute state, or dharmakaya. If you are able to abide in this state, effortlessly and free from subject and object, you are at the heart of the true nature and have obtained the heart of enlightenment. Abide in this great Dzogchen state and reactivate your beautiful motivation of bodhichitta and devotion, and the universe will appear as a magic show, a dream, a mirage. Presently, due to our habitual clinging to dualistic conceptions we have a strong sense of solidity, separation, and blockage. When we release all clinging, we will see everything as open, interconnected, and unobstructed.

What happens to the yogis and yoginis who practice and actualize this Dzogchen teaching? Their loving-kindness will become enormous. Their compassion will become unconditional. Their wisdom will be inconceivable. When we read about their life stories, we can see that many Dzogchen masters did not go to monastic colleges or engage in very much intellectual study; simply by meditating on the absolute state they spontaneously became great scholars. Their songs of realization are testaments to their profound mastery of the teachings. As your Dzogchen practice develops, your realization, wisdom, and intelligence grow, and your concern, care, and ability to help others also grow. The universe becomes magnificent—it has always been this way, and now you see it. You no longer hope to go to a pure land in the future to find nirvana. You no longer fear staying in samsara. Nirvana and samsara have merged into a single, beautiful natural state. When you have this realization, which is like sunlight dawning in the sky, rays, beams, and brilliant colors shine everywhere. When you discover the nature of your own mind, the universe unveils its glory to you.

Dzogchen masters have the highest realization, but at the same time their character and conduct is profound—the way they behave in the mundane world is so simple and pure. Effortlessly and spontaneously, everything they say, think, and do benefits all beings and themselves.

But beware of warning signs. If we boast about our realization, saying, "I'm a buddha, I'm an emanation, I'm a mahasiddha," or we broadcast our experiences, saying, "Last night I saw Buddha Shakyamuni, and this morning I spoke to Guru Padmasambhava," it is not good. If our arrogance increases, if our attachment thickens, if we blatantly disregard the rules of karma and disrespect others, we are moving in the wrong direction. Behavior like this is contrary to the Buddha's teachings and is not the way of a Dzogchen practitioner. It means the Dharma has not merged with our hearts, but only with our mouths. If this happens we must reduce the trade deficit and balance the budget! In other words, we must get back on track by applying the skillful means practices.

Up to this point, we have given instructions for the three levels of high capability Dzogchen practitioners. Whichever one of these instructions you practice, begin with genuine good heart motivation, reflect on impermanence, and generate devotion. Receive the lineage blessings, meditate on the true nature, and conclude with beautiful dedication and aspiration prayers. Then go into the world with these same thoughts and motivation.

# 13: Dzogchen Must Be Practiced

This Aro teaching focuses on meditation. It contains essential pith instructions on how to practice in order to attain realization. The Aro teaching is not a scholarly treatise. It is not a work of philosophy. It does not explicitly discuss the philosophical systems of Buddhism, such as the Abhidharma, Prajnaparamita, or Madhyamaka. These systems are of course very important—they are the very heart of what the Buddha taught. But in fact this Aro teaching is the essence of them all. The Aro teachings are concerned with how to identify, practice, and actualize the true nature of the mind, known as the "view." The philosophical systems of Buddhism we just mentioned, as well as all the Buddha's teachings, share this same goal. But the Aro teachings, just like the Dzogchen teachings in general, are the most direct and powerful.

It is very important to remember that Dzogchen is meditation. Study alone will not result in realization; Dzogchen must be practiced. And Dzogchen practice always includes the foundation practices. When we cultivate bodhichitta, awareness of impermanence, devotion, and appreciation for who we are and what we have, our minds become broad, stable, and strong. We will not hold extreme views. Then it becomes very easy to identify and abide in the natural state. As we continue to practice Dzogchen in this way, both the relative and absolute aspects of our view become increasingly wide and deep, until they are as vast and inclusive as space.

Although in the Aro teaching different practices are laid out to accommodate the abilities and experiences of different people, no one forces us to practice in a particular way. We should choose the practices that best suit us. The most important consideration is what promotes realization. We should select the practices that enable us to swiftly and efficiently reduce and eventually eliminate all habitual patterns, all grasping and clinging. It is also important to remember that no matter what practices we do, we should not exert too much forceful effort. Dzogchen is practice on the natural state, and the natural state is gentle and relaxing, as well as joyful.

# 14: Instructions for Medium Capability Practitioners of the Highest Caliber

Now we will discuss the teachings the great masters Aro Yeshe Jungne and Patrul Rinpoche have given for medium capability practitioners of the highest caliber. According to these great masters, people on this level should practice Dzogchen as the inseparable unity of shamatha and vipashyana.

*Shamatha* is a Sanskrit word that means "calm abiding." Shamatha is translated into Tibetan as *zhinay*. *Zhi* means "calm" or "peaceful," and *nay* means "abiding." So *zhinay* and *shamatha* both mean "abiding in a calm and peaceful state." This calm and peaceful abiding is one-pointed, or single-pointed; that is to say, it is very concentrated and not easily distracted. *Vipashyana* is also a Sanskrit word. In Tibetan it is translated as *lhagtong*. *Lhag* means "extraordinary," and *tong* means "seeing." Seeing with extraordinary vision—that is the meaning of *lhagtong* and *vipashyana*. Many people have translated *vipashyana* into English as "insight."

What is the extraordinary vision or insight of vipashyana? What is it that you see? With vipashyana you see everything that you see now. You see all the phenomena of the universe through the gates of your six senses. Nothing changes in that respect. But the difference is that with vipashyana realization, you also perceive the true nature of what you see. In other words, you see the reality of phenomena, which Buddhism calls "emptiness." When you see that things are emptiness it means you see that they are not solid; they are translucent and egoless. You see that things are always changing and moving, like waves or ripples of impermanence. You also see that everything is interconnected, so you are free from grasping and clinging to what you see. That is why this practice is called "seeing with extraordinary vision," or "insight."

The great master Patrul Rinpoche uses six quotations from the renowned

Kagyu teacher Yangönpa that embody the instructions for medium capability practitioners of the highest caliber:

1. The original nature should not be trapped by meditation.
2. The natural flow of mind should not be structured by conceptions.
3. Do not regard thoughts as bad.
4. Do not long for the nonconceptual state.
5. Abide in the natural state of mind with the assistance of mindfulness.
6. Meditate in this way, and you will arrive at the essence of calm abiding.

Regarding the last quotation from the great master Yangönpa, how long do you have to abide in the natural state? Patrul Rinpoche says that you must abide not just for a few hours, or for one day or a week—you must abide continuously. If you abide continuously with joyful effort, then the result will come naturally and beautifully. What is the result? Thoughts become increasingly less turbulent. The peaceful state of mind grows deeper and more expansive. This practice, as Yangönpa said, is supported by mindfulness. Every time you are distracted from the natural state, bring yourself back. If you continue like this you will achieve the perfect union of shamatha and vipashyana meditation.

# 15: Instructions for Medium Capability Practitioners of Medium Caliber

Now we will look at the teachings for medium capability practitioners of medium caliber. The Aro teachings say that for these people, the practice is the same as the one we just mentioned. You are going to abide with joyful effort in the natural state. You will notice that over time your conceptualizations, whether they are rough or smooth, big or small, will gradually wear away. In order to facilitate this more powerfully, while you are abiding in the natural state you should occasionally reactivate your feelings of closeness to Guru Padmasambhava, the buddhas, and the great masters. You should also reactivate love and compassion for all sentient beings, as well as appreciation for yourself. Invoke these beautiful thoughts, then continue abiding in the natural state.

If you reconnect with these beautiful qualities while you are abiding, and then allow them to merge back into nonduality, your practice will grow. You will experience and traverse the stages of samadhi, or meditation experience. The first stage of samadhi has five qualities:

1. Gross thoughts are still occurring.
2. Subtle thoughts are still occurring.
3. You are experiencing good physical sensations.
4. You are experiencing good mental sensations, such as peace and joy.
5. Your concentration is getting stronger, as is your ability to abide in the natural state.

As you continue to meditate with joyful effort, the second stage of samadhi comes. It has four qualities:

1. Your mind is becoming crystal clear.
2. Your concentration and meditation are more stable than before.
3. Gross and subtle thoughts are weakening in intensity—there is less mental turbulence.
4. You are becoming increasingly aware of your mind's activity.

By this time you have attained a very refined state. As you continue with joyful effort, you will reach the third stage of samadhi, which has five qualities:

1. Your mind and body are very comfortable, peaceful, and balanced. This is known as mental and physical pliancy.
2. You are happy mentally and physically. Everything feels good.
3. Your mindfulness is very strong.
4. You are very alert. You immediately detect movement within your mind and are able to liberate it, so you are not easily distracted.
5. Your concentration is very strong.

Finally the fourth stage of samadhi will come. It has four qualities:

1. Your mental state is balanced.
2. Your body is balanced.
3. Your mindfulness is strong.
4. Your concentration is strong, and your meditation is very powerful.

According to the Abhidharma, when you have achieved the fourth stage of samadhi you are free from the eight errors of meditation:

1. You are free from conceptions.
2. You are free from gross thoughts.
3. You are free from subtle thoughts.
4. Your breathing becomes so subtle that it no longer disturbs any of your body's energy systems.
5. You do not cling to physical pleasures.
6. You do not cling to mental pleasures.
7. You do not cling to uncomfortable physical states.
8. You do not cling to uncomfortable mental states.

The fourth stage of samadhi is the ultimate state. It is the highest stage of shamatha; it is also one with and inseparable from vipashyana.

The highest stage of shamatha *without* vipashyana can also be quite powerful. When your mind is more settled and refined, the turbulence of your conceptions decreases. Now the natural wisdoms radiate freely throughout your channels, and your intelligence quickens and expands. At this stage, omniscience can come quite easily. You can see and hear things from far away, even in different countries, and you can read the minds of others.

During the time when Guru Padmasambhava was in Tibet there was a practitioner named Nyang Tingdzin Zangpo who achieved this highest stage of shamatha practice very quickly. He could maintain one-pointed calm abiding meditation for weeks without being disturbed by conceptions, and he knew what was happening in India and China. But although Nyang Tingdzin Zangpo had attained these special abilities, he did not yet know the true nature of phenomena. Guru Padmasambhava said to him, "You have achieved the highest stage of shamatha, but you do not have realization of vipashyana." Guru Padmasambhava and the great master Vimalamitra then gave Nyang Tingdzin Zangpo instructions in Dzogchen meditation. He practiced them, attained vipashyana realization, and became one of the first Tibetans to achieve the wisdom rainbow body.

All Dzogchen meditation, including these instructions by Aro Yeshe Jungne, involves practicing the unity of shamatha and vipashyana. This is true even when the names "shamatha" and "vipashyana" are not explicitly mentioned. In Dzogchen, relaxing without focus and without distraction is shamatha, and seeing the true nature exactly as it is, is vipashyana.

# 16: Instructions for Medium Capability Practitioners of Lesser Caliber

Now we will discuss the practices for medium capability practitioners of lesser caliber. When you are meditating and your thoughts become restless, practice shamatha. In this case shamatha means to focus your mind one-pointedly on a single object. As soon as your mind is calm, release your mind from its object, and again rest your mind without focus. Resting the mind without focus is vipashyana. If while you are in the vipashyana state your thoughts once again become restless, go back to shamatha. Alternating between shamatha and vipashyana in this fashion will stabilize your meditation.

When the mind is wild and active you might think, "I'm not meditating very well." If you have such a thought, bring your mind directly to it. Look right into the heart of the thought, "I'm not meditating very well." The moment you do so, both the thought and the thinker dissolve. At that moment you are in the state where shamatha and vipashyana are one and inseparable, which is no other than the Dzogchen state.

Even if you can maintain this state for a few seconds or a few minutes, thoughts will return. So that you will not be carried away by those thoughts, reapply this technique. Look directly into whatever thought comes. Practice this technique with joyful effort and use it again and again.

Sometimes your mind is extremely distracted and nothing you can do in your meditation will stop it. In such cases you can stop your meditation for a short while and do a little physical exercise. At other times when you find yourself struggling with your meditation and perhaps trying too hard, you can loosen your posture, rest casually, and look into the sky.

Here is a technique you can use when your thoughts are really running wild: Think, "Okay, now I am going to think even more thoughts—thousands of thoughts, millions of thoughts—I am going to think every thought that has ever been thought!" Thoughts stop very quickly with this technique—it puts you right into the natural state. Another technique that is very useful is this one: when a thought comes, ask, "Where did this thought come from? Where is this thought staying? Where is this thought going?" Ask yourself any of these questions and you will find yourself in the nature of mind.

Again, when you are relaxing in the nature of mind, thoughts will come. Thoughts are the display of mind; they naturally arise. Great masters of the Buddha's teaching therefore do not see thoughts as something undesirable. They do not block or reject thoughts, and they also do not indulge thoughts. They continually abide in the natural state and simply let thoughts come and go. Thoughts in and of themselves are fine; grasping them as something real and important is what creates disturbances. A firm decision needs to be made. You need to decide that from this moment on you will not grasp thoughts, and that you will continually abide in the natural state. If you keep this decision in your heart and mind, and practice with joyful effort, each and every thought will be cornered and then dissolve into emptiness. This is known in Dzogchen and Mahamudra as the "self-clarity of mindfulness."

At this point Patrul Rinpoche quotes masters of the Drukpa Kagyu school who say that as you continually abide in this meditation, all distinctions and borders between thought and no-thought, or between movement of mind and abiding, will wear out and ultimately dissolve. If you continue practicing like this for about one month, your mind will become very sharp, and your day visions and night visions will merge. What does this mean? Day visions include all of your experiences that take place while you are awake. Night visions include all of your dreams that take place while you are sleeping. Right now you think your day visions are real and your night visions are not. But as you continue to practice in the way we just described, you will come to see that there is no difference between waking experience and dream experience. Day visions and night visions are both equally—indistinguishably—perceptions, and both are empty.

Here Patrul Rinpoche specifically quotes the great Drukpa Kagyu master Götsangpa, who said, "Do not meditate that perception is emptiness. Also, do not meditate that perception is not emptiness. Relax into the natural state of the mind. Whatever arises, let it be. When you relax into the natural state of the mind, you will eventually discover the nature of all your thoughts and perceptions. So do not conceptualize that things are empty. Relaxing into the natural state of the mind will take care of everything." If

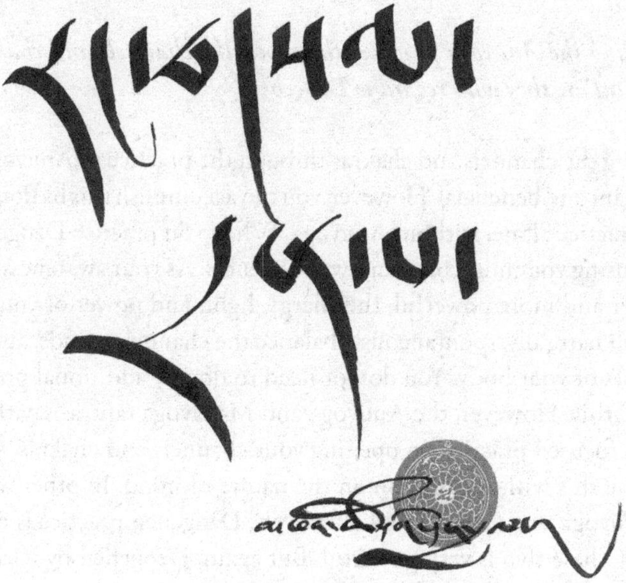

Self-Clarity of Mindfulness

you practice like Götsangpa said, in about a month you will begin to experience that everything is in the lucid state. This is the first stage of meditation experience, known as "free from complexity."

Summarizing this section of the teaching, master Patrul Rinpoche continues by saying, "Meditate on the nature of your mind." When you meditate on the nature of your mind you are meditating on the union of shamatha and vipashyana. You are simultaneously meditating on Prajnaparamita, Madhyamaka, Mahamudra, and Dzogchen. Again and again, look at your mind. Evoke the natural state and abide in it.

Many Dzogchen masters have said thoughts dawn as the light, or the light beams, of the nature of the mind. To witness the truth of this statement, it is important not to chase thoughts and not to think that thoughts are bad. Rather, look directly at the thought itself. The moment you look directly at the thought itself, the thought dissolves and merges into the nature of mind. That is an essential method of practice in Dzogchen.

If you have any questions we can discuss them now.

## Questions and Answers

*Regarding the Anuyoga practices that open the channels and chakras, how important are they with regard to Dzogchen?*

Opening the channels and chakras through the practice of Anuyoga is very important and beneficial. However, you can accomplish this by doing Dzogchen practice alone, without Anuyoga. When you practice Dzogchen, you are focusing your mind on your own awareness. As your awareness becomes stronger and more powerful, the energy, light, and power of your realization will naturally, spontaneously balance the channels, winds, and essence elements of your body. You do not need to do any additional practices to achieve this. However, the Anuyoga and Mahayoga tantras say that when you do focused practice on opening your channels and chakras, you must combine this with meditation on the nature of mind. In other words, for the Anuyoga practices to work effectively, Dzogchen practice is necessary. Uniting these two is very powerful. But again, Dzogchen by itself will do everything.

*I want to address the phrase "abide in the natural state." Doesn't the word "abide" encourage grasping? It says in the* Diamond Sutra *that the natural state is free from abiding.*

Yes, there is nothing to abide in. The *Lankavatara Sutra* says, "The true nature is free from names and labels." But in order to communicate we have to use some kind of terminology. The Buddha used words, and so do all the great teachers. The *Diamond Sutra* itself has three hundred verses of words. Yes, the true nature is beyond words and free from abiding. But in order to reach that state, words are necessary. Instructions spoken by masters help beings achieve realization. This does not mean the words themselves are totally true or free from flaws. The teaching explains that the true nature is free from thoughts, free from words, free from deeds, free from signs, and free from grasping. When the words that lead us beyond thoughts, words, deeds, signs, and grasping are absolutely understood by everyone, words will no longer be needed. But until then we need all kinds of words. Words usher us into the natural state. That is why the Buddha gave volumes and volumes of teachings. Without words, only practitioners of the highest capability can get realization. For this reason, great masters do not teach exclusively in silence. So although it is true what you say—that ultimately there is no abiding—words like "abiding" are necessary until realization is attained.

*Will Dzogchen practice help us in the bardo?*

Yes, Dzogchen practice will definitely help us in the bardo. In fact, if your Dzogchen meditation is strong now, you may not have to go through the bardo at all.

*In this Aro Yeshe Jungne teaching, are there specific techniques taught for the practice of shamatha?*

Yes. As you know, this Aro teaching has nine separate instructions. The instructions for lesser capability practitioners of medium caliber include specific techniques for shamatha. We will go over these shortly.

*Do the practices that open the channels require empowerment and instruction?*

Yes, to do the practices for the channels, as well for the winds and essence elements, it is necessary to receive empowerment and instruction. But again, Dzogchen practice, all by itself, will accomplish all of this.

*If we think of abiding, isn't that duality? How is thinking of abiding different from simply not abiding?*

That is true. Thinking of abiding is duality, and not abiding is duality too. To avoid these extremes, the teaching says that we should let the mind rest in its own natural state. This does not mean there is a substantially existing, solid natural state. Therefore we should not think of abiding, nor should we be distracted and not abide—we should simply abide. To abide is insubstantial. But again, while we are in duality, to get to that state, we have to speak in words.

*Who passed this Aro teaching that was arranged by Patrul Rinpoche to you?*

We received this teaching forty years ago, before the Communists invaded Tibet, from the master Khenpo Tenzin Dragpa. He was the headmaster of the shedra at Riwoche Monastery.

*The natural state is beyond duality, totally beyond the mind. In Zen Buddhism they call this the no-gate.*

Where is this no-gate? Is it open or closed? Which direction is this no-gate? North, south, east, or west? Or is it in the center? Ask the Zen master Bodhidharma, who created this no-gate? [Khenpo Tsewang Dongyal Rinpoche claps twice.] Here is the sound of two hands clapping. Do you see it? Do you hear it? I clapped. You saw it, you heard it. So again, where is the no-gate?

*Totally beyond the mind, right?*

If we play word games we can play for a long time.

*I'm not playing. I don't think you really understand me.*

I understand you. No-gate—I understand. When you say, "no-gate," and I say, "nonduality," these are similar, no? We're using different terms, but the meaning is similar, no?

*I want to speak so everyone understands. You have been talking about high, middle, and lesser capabilities. That is very dualistic. That is form. How is talking about form going to lead us to emptiness?*

What is the difference between form and emptiness? These words have different spellings and different sounds. What is the difference between them on the meaning level, in your mind?

*The difference between form and emptiness is that when you say nice things to me, I do not hear the meaning, I hear only sound. When you say bad things to me, I also hear only sound.*

So what is your question now?

*If I am beyond duality, if you say something I don't hear your meaning, I just hear the sound.*

I don't really understand.

*How can duality be part of the nature of the mind?*

Duality is part of the true nature too. But where does duality come from? It comes from emptiness. Right now duality is disturbing us. But the nature of duality is emptiness. There is no solidly existing emptiness, and therefore there is no solidly existing duality either. But even though this is true, we do not have realization, so we make distinctions. We have to get beyond our lack of realization and in order to do this we use different terminology.

*I think I understand. We have to go beyond duality to reach primordial mind—that is the first step. Then, when we reach primordial mind, we embrace the whole mind, which includes duality.*

Not exactly. The Dzogchen teaching says that there is no substantially existing, solid primordial mind. "Primordial mind" refers to awareness. This is not something that exists in a solid way.

*I am sorry, I am not trying to challenge Tibetan Buddhism.*

Everything is fine. In Tibetan Buddhist monasteries debate is very common. They ask and answer questions, back and forth. They challenge each other on many issues of Dharma. You're saying certain things, I'm saying certain things, and we are debating in small ways. In Tibet they do this a lot. They joke too, though sometimes it looks like they are arguing and fighting.

*You are the master, I am the student. I shouldn't debate with you.*

No, no, no. Masters and students debate, particularly in the academic institutes. This is not something to avoid—it is good to do. In the Zen tradition they don't debate too much; Zen is more direct. The masters give simple and profound instructions, and the students meditate on them. Then, if the students become drowsy when meditating, the masters whack them on the shoulders to wake them up. Some of our students have said to us that when they fall asleep during meditation, they wish we would do that!

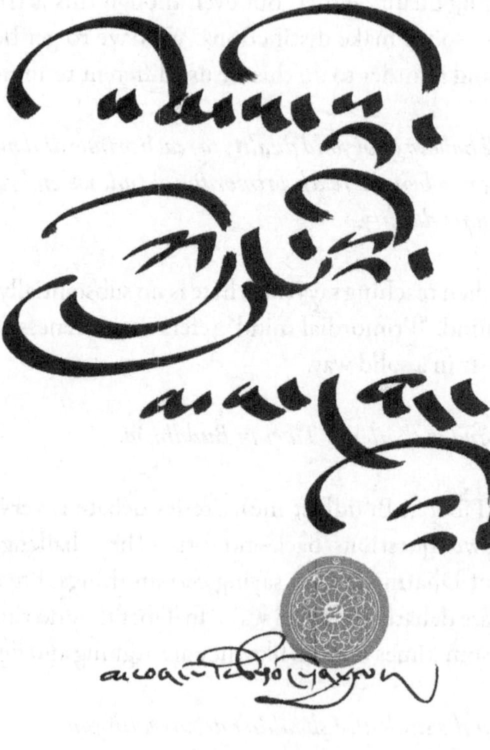

Semde, Longde, and Mennagde

# 17: Reminders

The Dzogchen teachings are divided into three sections: *Semde*, *Longde*, and *Mennagde*. These are translated into English as Mind Section, Space Section, and Essence Instruction Section. The teachings of Aro Yeshe Jungne contain some Space Section and Essence Instruction Section teachings, but they are mostly connected to the Mind Section.

What are the differences between these three sections of Dzogchen? There is very little difference. All three emphasize the practice of trekchö. What is trekchö? Trekchö is the practice we use to realize that all events and processes are naturally open, free, effortless, spontaneous, and perfect. Ultimately, the practice of trekchö comes down to letting go of clinging, not being distracted, and relaxing. The Mind Section emphasizes the practice of trekchö with regard to thoughts and emotions. The Space Section emphasizes the practice of trekchö with regard to all phenomena in the universe. The Essence Instruction Section emphasizes the unity, or inseparability, of the two.

All the Dzogchen teachings—however they are classified and named—are always based on a beautiful foundation that deals with the common world. As it says in this teaching, generate bodhichitta, reflect on impermanence, and feel the preciousness of your life and the opportunity you have to practice. Feel devotion toward the lineage masters and toward the teaching itself. We should lay this beautiful foundation firmly and deeply. This is the rich and stable ground we stand on as we deepen and expand our Dzogchen practice.

The foundation practices for Dzogchen are known as *ngöndro*, which means "preliminary." There are general ngöndro practices that begin with the "four reflections"—the precious human body, impermanence, karma, and samsara—and continue with taking refuge and generating bodhichitta. There are also ngöndro practices specific to Dzogchen, known as the outer and inner "Khorde Rushen," which are designed to redirect the mind toward the natural state. There are many different styles and techniques of ngöndro practice, but among them the most important are the ones we have been discussing throughout this teaching: bodhichitta, reflecting on impermanence, the preciousness of your life and opportunity, and devotion. Continue to cultivate these along with your Dzogchen meditation.

Now, when it comes to Dzogchen meditation itself, there is no focus. Although there is no focus, this does not mean that focus is bad. We are not against focus; we are not trying to negate or destroy it. Focusing, also known as "fixating," is a manifestation of duality. There is no substantially existing duality—duality is itself empty of self-nature, and the same is true of focus, or fixation. There is nothing to be against. It is all just wind moving through the sky.

In Dzogchen practice we do not negate or reject anything. We are practicing the true nature. The true nature is panoramic, all-inclusive, and beautiful. We do not recognize this because of our dualistic fabrications, grasping, and clinging. We have been doing this lifetime after lifetime, from beginningless time. We are wandering in samsara, and it is nobody's fault but our own. But now we release all dualistic fabrications, all grasping and clinging. We let go of subject and object. We relax our minds into the open sky state. The one who relaxes and the relaxation, also known as the meditator and the meditation, are a unity. Who is relaxing? Who is meditating? What is happening? There are no answers. This is nonduality. This is realization. This is Dzogchen.

In order to accomplish this state, the Buddha gave many different teachings. This teaching by Aro Yeshe Jungne includes nine different instructions that help us approach and accomplish the ultimate point, which is to abide in the natural state. Each of these instructions is complete and perfect; we should apply them according to our needs. Thus far we have gone over the first six. Now we will discuss the final three, which are designed for lesser capability practitioners.

# 18: Instructions for Lesser Capability Practitioners of the Highest Caliber, and the Five Stages of Meditation

Master Patrul Rinpoche says here that lesser capability practitioners may not understand the meaning of vipashyana at all. They might not have faith and trust in vipashyana. In some way, they might be uncomfortable and unfamiliar with the teaching. At the same time, their stability in shamatha practice is not strong. Even when they are sitting in good posture, their minds are easily scattered with conceptions and become dull, weak, and confused. In other words, for lesser capability practitioners, meditation—whether vipashyana or shamatha—does not come easily. Whenever this happens to you, ignite the skillful means or "appearance" practices, such as loving-kindness and compassion, joy, and appreciation. In other words, cultivate something positive and substantial that can be held in mind. Invoke these thoughts vigorously, and then sit down on your meditation cushion. Even if you are already sitting, renew the clarity of your body, speech, and mind. You can do this by reviewing and reapplying the seven postures of the Buddha Vairochana. These are as follows:

1. Sit cross-legged in the "vajra posture," or if you prefer, sit on a chair.
2. Sit up straight, with your neck bent slightly forward, so your entire spine is aligned.
3. Place your hands in the equanimity mudra, or place them palms-down on your knees.
4. Let the tip of your tongue gently touch the upper palate.
5. Keep your arms relaxed, with the elbows off the ribs.
6. Open your eyes and gaze toward the tip of your nose, or if you prefer, close your eyes.
7. Breathe naturally.

In this posture spend a minute or two clearing your mind—try to let all of your conceptions simmer down. Then do the breath purification exercise we do every morning. This exercise cleanses the three channels from impure winds associated with attachment, anger, and ignorance. After that, relax. Abide in the nature of mind without conceptions for a minute or two. Then in the sky in front of you—or if you prefer, above your head—feel the presence of your teacher in the form of Guru Padmasambhava. Guru Padmasambhava is the embodiment of all buddhas and teachers of the three times and ten directions. Feel strong devotion to him and recite the seven-line prayer as well as the prayers to the lineage masters and root teacher. Then, after praying, visualize that blessing lights come from Guru Padmasambhava, cleansing and purifying all your negativities, obscurations, and habitual patterns. Doubt, hesitation, dullness, weakness in meditation—these and all other hindrances to your realization are completely removed. Feel this very vividly. Then Guru Padmasambhava dissolves into light. This light enters your crown chakra, moves down your central channel, and enters your heart center where it merges with your awareness. At that moment let your mind look at your mind. What happens? The watcher and the watched merge, and there is no longer any subject and object. Now release your muscles and nervous system. Let everything go. Abide in the inexpressible nature of the mind, beyond categories and characteristics.

As you are relaxing in this state, suddenly thoughts will come up. As we said before, in the Dzogchen teachings thoughts are known as the display of the mind; they are the expressive energy of awareness. Do not regard thoughts as being bad. Do not prevent them, and also do not follow them. Let them come, be, and go. With regard to meditation experience, do not get excited over what might seem to be achievement, and do not despair over what might seem to be poor progress. These are just more thoughts. Instead of adding more thoughts, relax in the natural state. Do not expect good meditation; do not fear bad meditation. If dullness comes, reconnect to the energy of your awareness—re-invoke the clarity aspect of your mind. Let that power and its qualities arise anew, supported and checked by mindfulness. Employ any of these techniques as needed, with joy and devotion.

At times when you are practicing in this way, the surface of your mind may seem calm enough, but just below the surface, barely noticeable, are undercurrents of thought. Patrul Rinpoche here uses the metaphor "Underneath the hay there is running water." If the water is left unattended, eventually it will soak all the hay, at which point the hay will be useless. This is a metaphor for what can happen with the subtle, undercurrent thoughts. At first they might seem harmless, but if we do not attend to them they will grow stronger and disrupt—and possibly even ruin—our meditation. Therefore, when you notice undercurrent thoughts, you must increase your mindfulness. Meditation, from the top to the bottom, should be beautiful, clear, and calm. Bring up the clarity aspect of your mind and recognize the undercurrent thoughts. The moment you recognize them they are liberated. Once again, do not analyze or follow these thoughts. Just let them go.

There are times when you are meditating nicely, and suddenly your mind becomes busy and unstable. Your mind was peaceful and now it is wild. You might get upset with yourself and think, "Oh, I cannot meditate." When this occurs do not be discouraged. When you notice your thoughts increase and intensify, this is generally a sign of progress. The Dzogchen teachings say that there are five different experiences in meditation that signal development, and this is the first one. Your mind is like a stream running down a mountain. When a stream runs down a mountain, it moves swiftly. But even though your mind seems to be running very fast, actually below the surface it is slowing down. Your mind is actually calmer than it was before you started meditating, even if for the moment it may not seem so. How is this? Your mind has to become calmer to notice what it is doing. In the past, your mind moved all the time and you never even noticed; now you do notice. This is why you should not see this experience as failure but rather as something positive. You are more aware of your mind than before; this means you are improving.

Continue to apply the skillful means techniques of joy, devotion, and bodhichitta without boredom or fatigue, and with courage and commitment continue to meditate on the true nature. If you maintain your practice in this way with perseverance, you will reach the second stage of meditation experience: alternating stable and unstable experiences. Great masters compare this second stage of meditation experience to a water bird. This creature dives into the water and then after a few moments resurfaces to rest on a rock or a log. Then it dives back into the water and comes up again. It does this continuously.

At this time the training remains the same. Continue with the skillful means practices and meditate on the true nature. In time your mind will become more stable. It will occasionally move, but mostly when you meditate, the mind will stay in its own natural state. Patrul Rinpoche uses the analogy of an old man. An old man stays seated most of the time. Once in a while he gets up for a cup of coffee or tea, or maybe even to play golf, but otherwise he sits comfortably. There is not too much activity. By now your mind is like an old man. It does not move much, nor does it need to. This is the third stage of meditation experience.

Keep practicing as before. By now the surface of your mind is very smooth. Perhaps underneath the mind's surface there is slight movement, but otherwise you have attained good stability. Patrul Rinpoche uses the analogy of an underground river: the river still flows, but it is hardly noticeable. So what do you do now? You should invoke more mindfulness and energy. Why? By this time your mind has become very tame. It does what you want it to do; you have control and are not scattered at all. In the beginning, you had trouble with your restless mind—it was running wildly in every direction. It would not stay still for even a few seconds. But now you can rest.

Yet there is still the possibility of mind's becoming weak and dull. You can prevent this by invoking mindfulness and clarity. Apply the skillful means techniques and continue to meditate. Soon your mind will become very bright and stable, and you will maintain this state day and night without getting bored or tired. At this time, there is no particular desire for meditation, and no desire for belongings such as clothes. In the Dzogchen teachings this state is likened to a mountain. Your mind is unshakable—it cannot be moved by conceptions or perceptions. This is the fourth stage of meditation experience.

When you reach this stage you must continue to apply the skillful means practices and cultivate virtuous thoughts. Even though your mind has become very stable, do not ignore the power of loving-kindness and compassion, as well as joy, devotion, and appreciation. If you do not reactivate these skillful means practices at this time, you can get carried away by a blank, vague, dull state of mind that has no energy whatsoever. Also, there is still some subtle grasping and clinging that can erupt and create massive disturbances. You must continue to practice skillful means, and keep invoking the energy of mindfulness and clarity. Mind is not only empty—it is filled with many wonderful qualities. Unite this with emptiness meditation. Bringing this practice to the final state of complete fulfillment is the fifth stage of meditation experience.

These five different meditation experiences accurately describe the progress of most practitioners. People have varying abilities; they also have differences in the ways their channels are configured and how they perceive phenomena. This means that not everyone proceeds in exactly the same way. But most people will experience these stages pretty much in the way and order they have been explained.

# 19: Instructions for Lesser Capability Practitioners of Medium Caliber, Including Some Powerful Shamatha Techniques

For lesser capability practitioners of medium caliber, the following instructions are given in order to gain meditative stability. Maintain the same posture, and intensify the skillful means practices. Then right in front of you, about four cubits away, plant a small stick or twig in the ground so that it stands up vertically. A cubit is approximately the length of the forearm from the elbow to the tip of the middle finger. With strong concentration, unite your mind and your eyes, and look at the upper tip of the stick. This will stabilize your mind. Do not, however, focus too strongly—that will make you bored and tired. At the same time, do not be too loose—that will make you scattered.

In general, when you meditate you should be neither too forceful nor too loose. Avoid extremes and find balance. For this reason, the great wisdom dakini Machik Labdron said that if you are both strong and relaxed in your meditation practice, you will discover the essential point of the view. At first, do this practice on the stick in many short sessions with breaks. As your meditation experience grows you can do longer sessions with shorter breaks.

When your mind becomes more stable, you can change the practice by visualizing a white AH syllable on the upper tip of the stick and concentrate on that. If you prefer, you can visualize a small sphere of light on the upper tip of the stick instead of the AH. This sphere of light can be white, blue, red, yellow, or green—you can alternate. But do not change the colors too often—keep a single color for a day. Do this practice gradually, gently, and with balance to avoid the negative side effects we just mentioned.

If you feel you need to do more, replace the stick with small stones or marbles. Above the stones or marbles, you can visualize the white AH syllable or the small sphere of light in one of the five colors. When your mind becomes more stable and you wish to change the object of focus, then instead of visualizing spheres of light outside of yourself, you can visualize them on your forehead, speech, or heart centers. You can visualize the syllables from the Vajrayana teachings: a white OM on your forehead, a red AH on your throat, or a blue HUNG in your heart. Or you can simply stay with the white AH, visualizing it at any one of the three places. According to whatever makes your mind more stable and focused, you may apply any, some, or all of these techniques.

Whenever and however you meditate, be joyful. Do not neglect the skillful means practices. At the beginning of every meditation session—and even during the practice—invoke good thoughts. Again, do not be too forceful. But also do not back away and lose your courage, commitment, and confidence. If you are on a long retreat, during formal practice sessions, increase the strength and stability of your mind by maintaining good, balanced concentration on your object of focus. Then, during postmeditation periods, do prostrations and circumambulations. Perform meritorious activities such as building stupas or temples. Read books on the teachings, reflect on what you read, and absorb it into your heart. Cultivate love and compassion. All of these are the skillful means practices of the relative truth.

Relative truth and absolute truth are two aspects of the same nature. On the relative level, there are concepts and there is duality: subject and object, positive and negative, joy and suffering. Do not ignore this. Do not impose your realization of the absolute truth on the relative truth. At the same time, you should not use the concepts of the relative truth to try to figure out the absolute truth. That is playing games, and the absolute truth is not attainable through concepts. Cultivate wide-open wisdom that is nondual and free of concepts in order to experience the absolute truth. Unite this effortlessly and beautifully with the relative truth, and there will be no conflicts. Blend it all into a single state. This is how we stay focused, discover our innate nature, and benefit ourselves and others.

# 20: The Power of Mindfulness

You should always be mindful, not only during meditation but also during postmeditation periods. This means you should continually check yourself. "How is my mind?" "How am I behaving toward others and myself?" When you are mindful, you stay on course and open yourself to improvement. This is why Aro Yeshe Jungne, Patrul Rinpoche, and other great masters remind us again and again of the importance and power of mindfulness.

With regard to the practice of mindfulness, Patrul Rinpoche says that we should be "like a warrior in a sword fight," or "like a great beauty in a crowd." When in battle, a great warrior is absolutely focused. He knows that a moment's distraction can result in injury or even death. He has trained his mind to be unwavering, and does not allow any lapse in concentration during a battle. Similarly, before going out in public, a beautiful woman takes one last glance in the mirror. Then when she is among the crowd, she is confident and relaxed as everyone notices and admires her. As these analogies show, mindfulness preserves what you are doing and makes it even better. Therefore, apply mindfulness to your meditation practice.

# 21: Wisdom

Now we will talk about wisdom, which is realization of the true nature, or the absolute truth. Without wisdom, even if your conduct is perfect, you will not transcend duality. In the Prajnaparamita teachings, the great teacher Buddha Shakyamuni continually emphasized the importance of wisdom, saying, "If you do not have the sixth paramita of wisdom, the other paramitas are blind." The other paramitas are generosity, discipline, patience, joyful effort, and concentration; they are all beautiful. But without wisdom, they are not strong. Regarding the relationship of wisdom and the other paramitas, the Buddha said, "The wisdom paramita is like the universal king, and the five other paramitas are his retinue." The universal king needs a retinue to help him fulfill his wishes. The retinue needs the king because it needs a leader. The Buddha continued, "The sixth paramita of wisdom is the eye of all six paramitas." Accordingly, at the beginning of the ninth chapter in his *Guide to the Bodhisattva's Way of Life*, the great master Shantideva says that the Buddha gave all the many Prajnaparamita teachings so that we would actualize the sixth paramita. Later in that chapter, Shantideva says, "If you want to remove suffering totally, you must practice and attain wisdom."

To attain wisdom we must meditate on the true nature. But here the great master Shantideva cautions us: "Even though wisdom is so important, do not neglect the relative truth." This means that even if you have the highest realization of the absolute truth, you should not impose that realization when you are dealing with the relative world. You should be a decent person, and be sensitive and have respect for the capacities and understanding of others. For example, to tell a suffering person who has not trained in meditation, "But it's just a dream!" will not be at all beneficial and might even be harmful. Therefore, cultivate the unity of the two truths in your practice, but when you are in postmeditation and dealing with the common world and sentient beings, work within the system of the relative truth.

In order to quickly realize the unity of the two truths, in Vajrayana practice we visualize deities. In particular, in the inner tantras of the Vajrayana, we visualize male and female deities in union. The meaning of this visual-

SHANTIDEVA

ization is not what we might imagine it to be according to regular, mundane conceptions. This is a great secret teaching. The male deity symbolizes relative truth, the female deity symbolizes absolute truth, and their union symbolizes the unity of the two truths.

In the Vajrayana, the entire spiritual journey is laid out in terms of ground, path, and result. The ground, also known as the foundation, is the union of relative and absolute truth. The path, also known as the approach, is the union of skillful means and wisdom, or the union of the two accumulations of merit and wisdom. The result, also known as the achievement, or fruition, is the union of rupakaya and dharmakaya. *Rupakaya* means the "wisdom body of form or appearance," and it includes both the sambhogakaya and the nirmanakaya. *Dharmakaya* means the "wisdom body of emptiness." Ground, path, and result are therefore no other than the union of compassion and wisdom.

In this text we have been showing how this is practiced according to the Aro Dzogchen lineage. Here we will summarize the practices given for lesser capability practitioners of both the highest and medium caliber. When you have difficulty stabilizing meditation, first you should focus on and reactivate bodhichitta, reflect on impermanence, and generate devotion, joy, and appreciation. When your mind is stable and you are about to meditate on the true nature, assume the seven-point posture of Buddha Vairochana, do the breathing purification, and then relax in the nature of the mind. As the oral instructions mention, you can also visualize Guru Padmasambhava, chant the seven-line prayer and the prayers to the lineage, and invoke and absorb their blessings. Then dissolve the visualization into yourself and merge with the natural state.

Whenever you need to increase your mental stability, use the techniques that involve focusing on the sticks and syllables. These techniques will definitely make your mind more peaceful. When you practice, different experiences will come up, but do not let these experiences distract you. Remember to not be too forceful—that will make you bored and tired. Be relaxed and comfortable. Bring joyful effort, courage, and commitment to your practice. Strengthen positive thoughts and be mindful. Again, when it comes to meditating on the nature of the mind, abide in the state beyond conceptions, beyond grasping and clinging, and beyond duality, open and free. Afterward, dedicate the merit.

Do you have any questions?

## Questions and Answers

*Should we visualize Guru Padmasambhava above our head, or in the sky in front of us?*

It is up to you. Our dualistic minds might feel that visualizing Guru Padmasambhava in the sky in front is more familiar, or more reassuring. But the teachings also say it is good to visualize him above your head, facing the same way as yourself. Choose the one that is more comfortable and convenient for you—it is your choice.

*How do we invoke clarity?*

To invoke the clarity, cultivate joy, appreciation, loving-kindness, and compassion, and recite mantras. When you are meditating on the true nature, do not let your mental energy sink to the lower part of your body. Lift your concentration to the upper part of your body, even to your head. If you like, you can let it expand upward and outward, from your head into space. These are all good practices to invoke clarity.

*What does it mean when you see lights during meditation?*

According to the teaching, lights are the energy of clarity. When you see lights it means the clarity-energy of your mind is sparking. The nature of the mind—called *rigpa* in Tibetan—is very abundant. These lights are the display of rigpa's abundance. They appear due to different vibrations in your channels and energies, and external circumstances can also provoke them. Light is extensively discussed in Dzogchen, particularly in the tögal teachings. In general when you meditate, many different lights can appear: blinking lights like fireflies; lights that look like tubes, chains, and spheres; lights that seem to float or dart around; smoke-colored lights and lights of different colors; and all kinds of shimmering experiences. These are good signs. At the same time, we should not cling to them. Relax, meditate, and let your mind open to the vast, pure, instantaneous state. Do not analyze or follow these lights. Let them come, and let them go. But yes, lights are good signs.

*When I was meditating once, I heard my mother calling me although she was nowhere around. Is hearing sounds like this good or bad?*

That is okay since it is your mother's call! When you are meditating, various experiences like that will arise. It happens many times, in many different forms, and is neither good nor bad. But in this case, since it is your mother's call, it is good.

*What are the signs of being bored with meditation, and how can we fix that? Also, could you give more instructions regarding how to merge Guru Padmasambhava with your awareness?*

When you are bored with meditation you do not feel happy about doing it—you are almost dragging. If this happens, cultivate good thoughts. Reactivate your joy and appreciation. Reflect on the preciousness of your life and circumstances, and think of benefiting yourself and others. You have the time and the resources to accomplish something truly meaningful, so again acknowledge and embrace this fact. You can also read the life stories of great lineage masters or read the Buddha's teachings. This will bring you home, back to the starting place. All of this is beneficial and inspiring, and it will regenerate your interest in meditation.

Here are the instructions on how to merge Guru Padmasambhava with your own awareness: Visualize Guru Padmasambhava and chant the seven-line prayer and the Vajra Guru mantra. Then Guru Padmasambhava dissolves into a sphere of light, which enters your crown chakra and moves down your central channel into your heart center. At that point Guru Padmasambhava has merged with your mind and you do not have to visualize any more. Now you meditate on the absolute truth—that is, you do Dzogchen meditation. Relax in the natural state of mind. In the Vajrayana teachings this is called "completion stage meditation." Do this for as long as you can. During meditation thoughts will come. Let them come, and let them go. If you become distracted, bring your mind back to the natural state, assisted by mindfulness. Afterward, dedicate the merit. As we have said so many times, cultivate bodhichitta and reflect on the preciousness and importance of all life, including your own.

*We pray to the deities and ask them for assistance. Do the deities exist as beings external to us? How does this practice work?*

According to the Vajrayana teachings of Buddha Shakyamuni, Guru Padmasambhava, and other great masters, the deities are living buddhas even though we do not see them on the level of our dualistic perceptions. There are different buddhas living on different levels. Some are in pure lands and some are in different universes. These pure lands have different names, such as the pure land of Akanishtha, which is the pure land beyond duality. When you visualize and pray to a buddha, the visualization and prayer are conceptions generated by your mind, but there is a living buddha as well. This means that through the power of your mind in meditation, you invoke that living buddha's energy and blessings. Your visualization is like a photograph or a map. A photograph of a person is not the person; a map of a country is not the country. But there is an actual person and an actual country. The photograph helps you identify or remember the person, and the map shows you how to locate places within the country. Similarly, what you are visualizing and praying to is not the actual buddha, but through your visualization and prayer, you receive the energy and blessings of the actual buddha.

*The teachings say that when you attain enlightenment your mind merges with dharmakaya. The sambhogakaya and nirmanakaya forms are then emanated in order to benefit dualistic beings. I have heard that the sambhogakaya and nirmanakaya are ultimately the creations of sentient beings, reflecting their needs and aspirations. Is this true?*

Regarding the first part of your statement, your mind is always in the dharmakaya state. When you attain enlightenment there is nothing that you are merging into that is not already merged. This means that when you attain enlightenment, you realize what you have always been. In the Dzogchen teachings it says everything is in the dharmakaya state, but dualistic fabrications prevent us from seeing this. Therefore, the essential point is to be free of dualistic fabrications.

The Dzogchen teachings also say the nature of the mind is the embodiment of the three kayas. The dharmakaya is right here, so are the sambhogakaya and nirmanakaya. The three kayas, which are inseparable, are not something you obtain in the future. That is the first point.

After you attain enlightenment, due to your inspiration and aspirations, you emanate forms to benefit all sentient beings. These emanated forms are the rupakaya. The rupakaya includes the sambhogakaya and the nirmanakaya. The sambhogakaya is not perceived by sentient beings. In the Mahayana texts it says that one of the ways the sambhogakaya manifests is as the "five certainties." The first certainty is the perfect audience. The perfect audience is made up of highly realized beings not caught in duality. According to the bhumi system of the Mahayana, this audience is made up of tenth-bhumi bodhisattvas, which is to say, near-buddhas. According to the teachings, the sambhogakaya, in all its manifestations, is beyond duality.

Regarding nirmanakaya emanations, the Buddha used the example of a single moon reflected in many water bowls. This means that when we are ready and our devotion is strong, emanations of the buddhas appear to us. There is no limit to the number and variety of these nirmanakaya forms. Sometimes they appear in the form of a great teacher, sometimes in the form of an ordinary person, as a bird or a tree, or even as a sound—the possibilities are endless.

*Difficulties come up while we are on and off retreat. Is there a way to determine whether these difficulties are a sign that our practice is going well, or whether they are obstacles?*

The teachings say that during retreat, during daily practice, and during postmeditation periods, many hardships and obstacles can come and will come, and that you should take these as signs of achievement. Whether they are tangible or intangible, visions or dreams, or however they manifest, see them as positive signs or blessings. If you see them as blessings—even if they are not—they will in fact be blessings. If you do this, whatever hardships and obstacles you experience will become very positive. Although this is not always easy to do, if you perceive and transform difficulties in this way, your practice will go very smoothly and beautifully, and you will deepen and expand your meditation power.

# 22: The Four Renunciation Thoughts

On every level of the teachings, from the Hinayana up to and including Dzogchen, Buddha Shakyamuni, Guru Padmasambhava, and other great masters say that if we want to attain enlightenment it is important to recognize, appreciate, and treasure what we have and what we are. This is the first renunciation thought; it is called the precious human life. To be born as a human being is very precious and as rare as a star in the daytime. Even if we cannot always see them with our eyes, there are far more beings in the hell, hungry ghost, god, and asura realms than there are in the human realm. In modern times the human population is growing, but the number of humans is still quite small compared to the number of these other beings. This means that simply to be a human being is unique and special. The Buddha's teaching also says that within the human realm, those who treasure genuine love, compassion, and wisdom and truly want to help others are very rare. Such persons possess the eighteen qualities of the precious human birth. They are the rarest of the rare.

Everyone in this room has these eighteen precious qualities. We are among the rarest of the rare. We also have a considerable degree of freedom and leisure. At this moment we are here, together, in this beautiful retreat place, studying and meditating on the Dzogchen teachings. This is not accidental and it is not random—it has manifested due to many beautiful causes and conditions. We should use this opportunity wisely to bring even more beautiful things to ourselves and others, and fulfill the meaning and purpose of our lives. That is what the teachings say that we should do. But it is not enough that the teachings say it. We must see and experience it for ourselves. We must take the time to really reflect on our lives and circumstances. We have so many reasons to be happy and grateful. We are beautiful, intelligent beings; we have compassion in our hearts; we have the teachings and teachers; and we have the time and resources to practice. We can become buddhas and help others to become enlightened as well. This is cause for tremendous joy.

The second renunciation thought is impermanence. When we look closely at our environment and the beings within it we see that everything and everyone is changing. Nothing stays the same—including ourselves. This is the way nature is, the way of relative truth. The teachings say that among all conceptions, the supreme conception is impermanence. In other words, thinking of impermanence is the best, most useful thought, because it is the most truthful.

As an example of impermanence, we can look at the movement of time. January merges into February, February becomes March, and like this the months keep passing through December until the year ends. January returns, and with it another year begins that will also end. On and on like this it goes. Time moves swiftly. This is also true for individual beings. It has been said many times that the span of a single life is like a book with a finite number of pages. Each page we turn brings us closer to the end of a chapter, and a new chapter begins. Right now we are in this chapter. We should read every word with care so that when we finish it our hearts and minds are full of wisdom. Then we can begin the next chapter bathed in brilliant, beautiful sunshine. That is our plan, and that is the purpose of the teachings and the practices.

Time is wonderful and precious and limited, and it is in your hands. Use it well, as all the great masters did before you. With courage and commitment, continue your practice. Do not waste this opportunity. Of course, we have many things to do in the relative world, but along with these, we should develop our inner strength and realization. We should develop internally at least as much as we do on the external level, and perhaps the internal level should be emphasized even more. Therefore, please reflect on impermanence. It will strengthen your joyful effort and motivate you to strive for and attain what is positive and everlasting. When you appreciate the power of your time and acknowledge its fleeting nature, you will not waste it; you will use it well. Then, when your time ends—when the book of this life is finished, and your body and mind separate—you will not be disappointed.

The third renunciation thought is karma. Karma means that whatever we do comes back to us. When we love, love is returned to us. When we hate, we receive hate in return. That is the internal system of karma. The process is the same in the external karmic system. When we plant rice seeds, we get rice. When we plant corn seeds, we get corn. Everything manifests according to its causes and conditions, which create inevitable results. This is not Buddhist dogma; it is a law of nature. It is important to contemplate this so we know what is good and what is bad for ourselves and others. Even an action that appears insignificant can have enormous consequences. Please be intelligent regarding karma, and very careful with your actions, because a tiny seed can bear a lot of fruit.

When we are fully aware of the inevitability of karma we empower ourselves. We all want happiness; no one wants suffering. Karma teaches us that positive actions bring positive results, which lead to happiness, and negative actions bring negative results, which lead to suffering. A combination of positive and negative actions brings results that are a mixture of happiness and suffering. What is the source of negative and positive actions? The great master Nagarjuna said that actions based on ignorance, attachment, and anger are negative, and actions based on wisdom, nonattachment, and loving-kindness are positive. This means that we create our own karma by what we think, say, and do—we are the agents and creators of our happiness and suffering. Taking this to heart, we should work continuously to uproot all our negative mental tendencies and to cultivate and glorify the positive ones. We should continually manifest this in our words and actions for ourselves and others. This is the way to properly work with karma, even if we are practicing Dzogchen.

The fourth renunciation thought is that samsara is unsatisfactory, frustrating, and full of suffering. Samsara begins with dualistic mind. At the heart of dualistic thinking is ego-clinging: the strong sense of being an "I" who is separate and more important than everyone and everything else. Dualistic mind is always accompanied by its retinue of the five negative emotions: attachment, anger, arrogance, jealousy, and ignorance. Ignorance, in particular, manifests as doubt and hesitation, and in narrow, carefully guarded intellectual stances. Dualistic mind puts an enormous amount of time and energy into supporting, strengthening, and defending itself. It judges situations only in terms of its own hopes and fears. It is sensitive, wary, and easily wounded. It is never satisfied.

The activities of dualistic thinking are known as samsara. Samsara means "circling" or "wandering." This means that no matter how much we think, speak, or act based on the demands of our dualistic mind, we never really get anywhere. The more effort we put into samsara, the more frustrating it becomes. Eventually we fall into a pit of suffering.

When the Buddha gave his first teaching on the four noble truths, the first truth he taught was the truth of suffering. He taught that suffering is painful, but we can learn from it, use it wisely, and ultimately go beyond it. We can learn from our own suffering to be more compassionate to others who also suffer. We can use our suffering as a catalyst to bring more courage, commitment, and joy to our practice. As our practice deepens, our minds grow in strength and clarity so that we can penetrate to the cause of suffering—dualistic mind—and transform and transcend it. When we are absolutely free of samsara we can help others become free as well.

The complete meaning of the fourth renunciation thought is that while samsara is painful, it can and should be used for understanding and realization. The Mahayana and Dzogchen teachings say that samsaric situations are agents of our transformation and growth, and that the greatest suffering, when worked with intelligently, yields the greatest realization.

These four renunciation thoughts are also called the "four attitudes that reverse the mind," or the "four thoughts that turn the mind toward the Dharma." These four thoughts accurately depict the relative truth. When we reflect deeply on them, we will no longer have any delusions. We will know how nature functions. We should know who and what we are. We are looking to the past, looking at the present, and most important, looking to the future. Life is so precious and fleeting. What we do echoes back to us. Samsara—which is dualistic mind—is unsatisfactory; it can be transcended.

In Dzogchen it says that it is good to thoroughly investigate the relative world. Train your mind to see, bring what you see into your heart, and with this understanding as your ground and foundation, build your practice. Once the relative truth is thoroughly comprehended, it becomes much easier to identify and abide in the absolute truth.

# 23: Realizing Absolute Truth

Dzogchen is ultimately meditation on the absolute truth. At the present time you might have glimpses of the absolute truth, but only briefly, because your mind is still involved with thoughts. We have been investing in these thoughts for a long time. As a result, in the beginning stages of practice, recognizing absolute truth can be maintained only for a short time. Without even realizing it, we are thrown back into our world of thoughts. In other words, in the beginning stages of practice, dualistic mind is more familiar and comfortable, so it is inevitable that we will continually return to it.

Because of the strength of our habitual patterns, we should meditate on the absolute truth with great joy, devotion, and bodhichitta, and with courage and commitment. Whenever we practice with these skillful means, we will experience glimpses of the absolute nature. As we continue in our practice, these glimpses will become longer in duration, and they will become more stable, strong, and natural. In time we will be able to maintain the view of the absolute truth without being disturbed by any relative turbulence, and we will no longer revert to dualistic mind. Even if your experience of the profound nature of the absolute truth is fleeting now, if you cultivate great joyful effort and keep practicing, it will expand and deepen. The fabrications of dualistic mind will decrease, and your realization will grow stronger. Eventually, dualistic mind will completely dissolve and absolute truth will be all that remains.

What are the characteristics, or qualities, of the absolute truth? The moment after his enlightenment, Buddha Shakyamuni said, "The true nature I have discovered is profound, peaceful, free of complexities, clear light, and uncompounded." What did he mean? "Profound" means infinite and powerful. "Peaceful" means calm and soothing. "Free of complexities" means transcending all thoughts and emotions. "Clear light" means instantaneous and perfect understanding of all phenomena. "Uncompounded" means simple and complete.

These are the qualities of the profound nature of pure awareness, the absolute truth, the Dzogchen view. Since this realization is beyond dualistic mind, it is difficult to understand. For this reason, moments after his enlightenment, the Buddha said, "Perhaps I should stay silent, alone in the forest, and not tell anyone of my realization." As soon as the Buddha spoke these words, the gods Brahma and Indra appeared before him. Brahma offered the Buddha a thousand-spoked golden wheel, and Indra offered him an auspicious conch shell. Together they urgently requested the Buddha to turn the wheel of Dharma and teach others. The Buddha accepted and began to teach, first at Sarnath in Varanasi, and then at other places.

Dzogchen is the Buddha's highest teaching of the absolute truth. It introduces the nature of the mind directly, without any sidetracks or detours. In order to realize the Dzogchen teaching, first cultivate bodhichitta, devotion, and the other skillful means practices. Then, when you practice Dzogchen meditation itself, you identify and relax into your own natural state of mind. When you relax into the natural state there is nothing substantially existing that you are relaxing into, and no substantially existing person who is relaxing. It is beyond subject and object, beyond actor and action. All these merge into a single state—the natural state. Even though we use the word "merged," there is no "merger" and there is no "merging." Once you have a glimpse of this state, you have to maintain it with joyful effort; otherwise this realization can easily become blurred with conceptions. But when conceptions come, do not see them as obstacles. Simply maintain awareness. You will observe that conceptions naturally dissolve by themselves.

# 24: The Aro Lineage and the Nine Levels Revisited

Earlier we traced the Aro lineage in a very specific way, beginning with Aro Yeshe Jungne himself. If we trace the Aro lineage as being one with and inseparable from the complete Dzogchen lineage—which it is—then it begins with Buddha Samantabhadra, who represents the true nature of awareness, infinite and ever-present enlightenment. Samantabhadra manifested in nirmanakaya form as Guru Padmasambhava and Vimalamitra. Guru Padmasambhava passed the lineage to the wisdom dakini Yeshe Tsogyal. From Yeshe Tsogyal it passed to Aro Yeshe Jungne. After Aro Yeshe Jungne, an oral transmission lineage developed which eventually came to Longchenpa in the fourteenth century. Longchenpa passed the lineage to Jigme Lingpa, who passed it to Gyalwai Nyugu, until finally it was passed to Patrul Rinpoche. We received the lineage from Khenpo Tenzin Dragpa, and now have passed it to you.

How will you take full advantage of the Aro lineage? You should see which level of practice is best suited to you. For many people it will be advantageous to start with the lowest capability practice and travel upward. This is a way to build a strong foundation in an organic fashion. It is also possible to start with the highest capability practice. The teachers will not put a high, medium, or lesser tag on you and impose a practice. You must decide, based on your own wisdom. Do not lock yourself into a single category as if it were a prison. You might be capable of practicing at the highest levels but discover that at certain times and in certain situations the techniques of a so-called lower level are necessary and useful.

The nine levels and the instructions that correspond to them in the Aro teaching are not completely different from one another. They are all related and support one another. At the same time, each one by itself is a perfect Dzogchen teaching that if practiced with joyful effort will lead to complete

LONGCHENPA

realization. In the Buddha's teaching—from the Hinayana all the way up to Dzogchen—the true nature is always the same. There are, however, different methods to actualize the true nature. As we said, the great masters of the Nyingma school of Tibetan Buddhism arranged all the methods the Buddha taught into nine yanas, or vehicles. There are other schools of Buddhism, each with its own way of categorizing the teachings, and there are many forms of Buddhist practice. All of this variety and difference exists only in terms of how to reach the goal; it doesn't refer to the goal itself. There is only one goal.

# 25: Instructions for Lesser Capability Practitioners of Lesser Caliber

We return now to the actual Aro teaching. Here it says that if you have tried the eight instructions given up to now, and still your mind is unstable and your thoughts are disturbing, you should practice like this: When the next thought comes up, look at it. Ask yourself, "Where did this thought come from?" As soon as you ask yourself this question, you arrive at the natural state. Once you are in that state, try to abide in it for a few moments. As an alternative, you can ask, "Where is this thought going?" or "Where is this thought abiding?" Another question you can ask when a disturbing thought arises is, "What is the nature of this thought?" Any of these questions will lead you directly to the natural state. Use whichever question you like, but once you reach the natural state you do not need to ask any more questions—simply abide. If you practice like this, over time you will not even have to ask a question. You can simply look at the disturbing thought, and it will dissolve. With a bit more practice, your realization of the true nature will become more stable, and thought will release itself by itself. At that time you will not have to do anything to abide in the natural state.

We are talking about the natural state of your mind, as well as the natural state of the minds of each and every sentient being. The natural state is beyond all ideas and emotions, as well as all striving and attaining. That is why it is known as "free from complexities." Freedom from complexities is within you—it is you; it is your own true nature. Your own true nature does not solidly exist, and so it is called "emptiness." This emptiness is not a blank or vacant state of mind. It is all-knowing and all-compassionate. It transcends everything, and it is prior even to time and space. Therefore it is known as "primordial wisdom." Primordial wisdom is indestructible and cannot be altered, no matter how deeply entrenched in samsara you are. Among everything, it is the most valuable. For this reason, it is called "vajra," or "diamond." It sees without any biases, preconceptions, or selfish motives. Since it experiences everything with absolute clarity, it is called "pristine awareness." Who created this pristine awareness? No one created it. That's why it is called "self-born wisdom."

In another teaching, Patrul Rinpoche says that you do not have to travel to another place to discover the nature of your mind. Your mind is wherever you are. Why go somewhere else, when your mind is already here? Nor do you have to consult another person. It is your mind. When you are happy or sad, do you have to ask someone, "Am I happy?" or "Am I sad?" Of course not; you know clearly how your mind is doing. This natural capacity to know your own mind is called "self-knowledge," "self-luminosity," or "self-clarity." It is also simply called "intelligence." Here the Aro teachings say that you should apply this natural capacity right now. Use your intelligence and look within—look at your own mind. When you do this, you do not see any subject or object. You do not see anything in particular. You go straight to the nature of your mind.

Realization is not far off. You can experience a glimpse of realization right now. Look at your present thought and ask, "What is the source of this thought?" This present thought is sometimes called "ordinary thought," or "ordinary mind." The moment you look for the source of this present thought, it immediately becomes something extraordinary—pristine awareness. Realization is your nature, and your nature never leaves you. It is ever-present and available. You can transform duality into nonduality at any time, even this very instant if you wish. Patrul Rinpoche says that this is due to the unimpeded nature of the mind.

This is your original mind. From this pristine true nature of rigpa, conceptions emanate. Chains or strings of thoughts keep coming. Yet this original mind is free from thoughts, even while it is their source, abiding place, and destination. It is the same teaching again and again: look within your own mind, understand its nature clearly, then maintain this realization. This is how to practice on the nature of the mind.

Once you get a glimpse of this realization, full realization is inevitable if you keep practicing. Keep up this meditation without any effort or force. The true nature is very relaxed, so we should be at ease when we are abiding in the natural state. Also, we should not try to structure anything with thoughts. This creates forcefulness, tightness, and regimentation—precisely the opposite of the true nature. Let all thoughts come and go, and be open. When we relax in this state, we can enjoy the nectar of the true nature as it is. This is good for us and good for others, and through this we can reach enlightenment.

Of course, during the beginning stages of practice, when you have a glimpse of realization, it is hard to maintain for a long time. We all know this. Therefore joyful effort and mindfulness are very important. The goal is to sustain awareness. Keep this goal in mind and practice with enthusiasm. Do not neglect the other components of practice, such as devotion to the lineage masters and to the teaching, as well as bodhichitta, joy, and appreciation. Even though these are conceptual, they are skillful means practices, and always good for us. Skillful means are part of the true nature—they are relative truth, which is inseparable from absolute truth.

When you practice like this, if your thoughts are still disturbing you and will not be pacified, if you are alone, you should relax your body. Do not do the seven postures of Buddha Vairochana. Sit in a free style, or perhaps even lie down. Make yourself comfortable, and apply the technique of opening your mind and observing it without restriction. Let thoughts come, however many there are. Let them move about as they like. When they want to go, let them go. If you do this, all of the turbulence will subside, and you will experience the peace of the natural state.

If you prefer, you can use another technique. In this second technique you try to increase the busyness of your mind—try to produce more and more thoughts. Do this, and within moments your mind will just stop; once again you will discover the natural state. Whenever you use one of these two techniques, do so gently, in an unstructured way.

When you have regained stability in the natural state, return to sitting in a formal posture. Try to maintain this state. Observe how your mind actually functions. When a single thought comes, or when many thoughts come, they do not go anywhere. They come from the natural state, abide in the natural state, and return to the natural state. They never leave the natural state. Here Patrul Rinpoche uses an analogy taken from a Dzogchen tantra. In ancient times, when sailors sailed the ocean, they always took crows. When the sailors traveled for a long time and wanted to know if they were approaching land, they would release one of the birds. If the crow came back it meant that land was still far away. Thought is similar to a crow released from its cage, flying high and fast in search of land that is not there. When a thought appears, it looks for a moment as if it is going somewhere. But where does it go? It goes back to where it came from—the natural state of mind.

That was the teaching about where thought comes from, where it abides, and where it goes. Now we look at thought itself. Thought itself is transparent, lucid, and empty. If a thought comes, it is empty. If it stays, it is empty. If it goes, it is empty. Thought is never separated from the natural state. Therefore, relax in the natural state as it is.

Although it may be difficult in the beginning, if you continue to practice in these ways, soon you will be able to relax your mind in the natural state quite easily. You will also be able to remain in the natural state without grasping, no matter what thoughts arise. This has been the teaching for lesser capability practitioners of lesser caliber. We have now completed the instructions for all nine levels of practitioners.

Do you have any questions?

## Questions and Answers

*Marpa was a great master, but when his son died, he was sad. How does that relate to Dzogchen realization?*

It is true, Marpa was upset—he was very close to his son. Other great masters have gone through similar things. When you have realization of the absolute truth, you are not immune to feeling—you are still part of the relative truth. In this case, Marpa was sad when his son died; he also felt sorrow for his other family members who were grieving. But Marpa's experience, just like the experience of all great masters, is very different than ours. They may appear to be sad or suffering, but what they are experiencing is actually much more playful.

*The true nature of mind is emptiness. But then who is it that recites the prayer in the ngöndro, "May my mind turn toward the Dharma?"*

It is true that mind is emptiness. But even though your mind is emptiness, right now you do not recognize it. At this time your mind turns to its dualistic thoughts. When you recite this ngöndro prayer, you are praying that your mind turns toward the Dharma instead. In particular, your mind needs to understand more about the importance of the relative, skillful means practices such as loving-kindness and compassion. The more you ignite these qualities, the less interested you are in your dualistic thoughts. As you continue to pray for more realization of the relative truth, your dualistic mind gradually stops interfering with your realization of the absolute truth, and eventually you fully realize emptiness.

*By studying and reciting the* Heart Sutra, *I understand that we might reach a point where we no longer grasp at the conception of pain. How will that affect our experience of actual physical pain? What suggestions do you have regarding dealing with physical pain?*

When you realize the teaching of the *Heart Sutra*, you remove the cause of suffering and pain—you are free from karma and negative emotions. For this reason, good practitioners may appear to be experiencing suffering, but their suffering and pain is not like ours. It is magical and dreamlike. The great future Buddha Maitreya taught in the *Uttaratantra*, "Realized beings who are free from karma and emotions do not experience suffering and pain as ordinary beings do." It is the same when realized beings enjoy one of the objects of the five senses. For these beings everything is a magical display, or like a dream. Even if it seems like they are experiencing great pleasure, their pleasure is different than ours would be in similar circumstances. Why? Because for realized beings there is no grasping and clinging.

How should you handle suffering and pain? The Buddha taught a variety of techniques on how to turn the experience of pain into Dharma practice and make it positive. Of course, suffering and pain are not good. When you experience suffering you are reminded of how bad it is. At the same time, you can reflect on the fact that so many other beings are enduring similar and maybe even worse difficulties. Use this understanding to ignite your loving-kindness, compassion, and wisdom. Pray, "May my present hardship be the cause that frees all beings from suffering and its causes."

The Buddha's teachings also mention that whenever you experience suffering and pain, your negative karma is being burned. This negative karma was latent within your mind; it was inevitable that you would experience it and now it has manifested. In this way, suffering and pain, rather than being bad, are actually good. They are a powerful detergent that cleanses and purifies you. You can think, "This is positive. I am ridding myself of negative karma. Better now than later. It will hasten my realization."

Finally, on the absolute level, what are suffering and pain? They are emptiness. And who is experiencing these? Your mind, which is also emptiness. Look directly at the suffering and pain, and then look directly at yourself.

At that moment you release and transcend the experience and the one who experiences. Then simply relax in the natural state of the mind.

*Is pain the physical sensation, and suffering the way the mind reacts, interprets, and clings to this sensation?*

Yes. Dualistic mind is regimented. It labels and divides experience, then grasps and clings to certain parts. It fixates on these, and ignores or devalues everything else. When you do not grasp and cling to your pain and suffering in any way but see them as part of the display of the true nature and integral to your spiritual growth, you deepen your practice.

*The body might suffer, but why should the mind also suffer?*

That's true. If the body is suffering, why should the mind be uncomfortable? Body and mind will go their separate ways sooner or later. The body is temporary, but mind is not. It's the same for a house and its tenant. If the house wears out why should the tenant be sad?

*Does karma mean that the past creates the present, so that whatever happens had to happen? Is there only one possible way things can go? Do we have a choice? Can we alter karma?*

"Karma" is a Sanskrit word that means "action," which in Tibetan is *le*. For example, we are here today to discuss the teachings because of our actions—we did what was necessary to get here. When the teaching is over and we leave, that is also our action. So karma is our actions and their consequences.

We often think that whatever we are experiencing in the present is entirely rooted in the past, but this is not always the case. Not everything comes from the past—the past is only one component of karma. There is also the present and the future to consider. The laws of karma are complex and profound. Only enlightened beings can understand them precisely. The Buddha divides karma into three categories:

1. The results of past karma, which are the experiences of this life caused by actions in past lives.
2. Causal karma, which refers to the actions of this life that will cause experiences in future lives.

3. Present karma, which refers to present experiences that do not have heavy consequences.

We should not overemphasize the past when we think of karma. It is important, but the present is even more important. We should perform virtuous actions right now.

*There are three metaphors for the liberation of thoughts and emotions that are mentioned in the Dzogchen teachings: "meeting an old friend," "a snake unknotting itself," and "a thief entering an empty house." How do these correspond to the three levels of capability among Dzogchen practitioners?*

The lesser capability practitioner's way of liberating a thought or emotion is like meeting an old friend. A thought or emotion appears, it triggers some kind of reaction, but then you recognize the situation and remember to release it. That is the way a lesser capability practitioner handles and liberates thoughts and emotions. The snake unknotting itself is a metaphor for medium capability practitioners. In this case, the liberation or release occurs more spontaneously. Finally, for high capability practitioners, the thought or emotion liberates according to the metaphor of a thief entering an empty house. A thief who enters an empty house immediately sees that there is nothing to steal, and instantly leaves. For all three of these approaches, once liberation happens the result is the same, but the way of liberation and the time it takes are slightly different.

*When a thought or emotion arises, is it important to know which of the three categories of karma produced it?*

It is not necessary. But we should know that good activities bring good results. For this reason, the teachings say that if you want to know your past karma, look at your present situation. If you want your future to be good, act positively now.

*When hardship comes, is it because of past karma? How should it be handled?*

Yes, our difficulties may be due to past karma, at least partially. But whether the cause is past karma, or both past and present karma, the best way to handle the situation is through purification, which means to increase the positive. Add more meditation practice, virtuous activities, and good thoughts—in other words, apply the teachings. Difficulties are not bad; they are reminders of samsara and can motivate us to increase our love and compassion. By facing difficulties we can transform ourselves. There are many teachings on this topic. For example, the teachings say that hardship and suffering are more beneficial to spiritual growth than happiness and pleasure. Pleasurable circumstances can easily lead to pride and complacency, while hardship can spur us on the path. Many great masters sang songs about hardship and suffering, referring to them as blessings and signs of achievement. So accept difficult situations, do good practice, and perform virtuous deeds. This will help cleanse and purify the causes of pain and sorrow, and create a powerful momentum that will speed us toward realization.

*If someone who has never studied or practiced Dzogchen asks us about it, can we talk about it? How much can we tell them?*

You can talk about Dzogchen. You can say that Dzogchen is the union of unconditional love, compassion, and wisdom. You can say that Dzogchen means going beyond thought, and no longer grasping and clinging to negative emotions. It might be better not to discuss actual practices, such as analyzing the source of thoughts, where they abide, and their destination. It also might be better not to mention that in Dzogchen, pain and suffering are liberated into the absolute nature. Of course these are true, but it may be difficult to explain this to someone unfamiliar with Dzogchen. Even if you explain it quite well, misunderstanding can easily occur. It is better to discuss Dzogchen from the perspective of boundless love, compassion, and wisdom. This approach is always beneficial.

*Can you say a little bit more about the relationship of emptiness and clarity regarding the nature of the mind, and how this applies to meditation practice?*

The nature of the mind is emptiness. But mind is not just emptiness; it is also clarity. The clarity aspect of mind has many qualities, among them love, compassion, and wisdom. Emptiness and clarity are in union. To practice the clarity aspect of mind, cultivate boundless love, compassion, and wisdom, and share this with all beings. As you do this, look directly at your mind—mind is empty. At that point, simply relax. If you combine clarity and emptiness in your practice, you will discover the nature of your mind, which is the nature of everything.

*Sometimes when I meditate, I get to the nonthought state, but then it gets a little dull. When I try to bring more clarity, it gets a little tense. What should I do?*

There are different techniques. For instance, you can send a deep breath out into space. Or you can use different syllables, such as PHAT. Shout PHAT fast and strong, like a shooting star. Both of these techniques instantly bring you back to the state of freshness. Perhaps it is best to shout PHAT when you're alone, and send a deep breath out into space when you are with others.

*I experience thoughts moving to and from the natural state, but when they are present they seem so solid. What can I do to make them seem less solid?*

Again, when you are alone, shouting PHAT is very effective. Use it strongly, powerfully, without planning or hesitating. Instantly shout PHAT—it brings you right back to the natural state. The actual meaning of the word PHAT is "cutting through." The meaning and the sound of PHAT are the same. When you shout PHAT, it instantly cuts through and clears the turbulence of your mind. It shatters the seeming solidity of your thoughts. Shouting PHAT brings you back to the natural state immediately. Once you return to the natural state, simply stay there. Shouting PHAT is an important and renowned Dzogchen practice.

# 26: Practicing the Two Truths to Realize the One True Nature

When you practice Dzogchen you are practicing every aspect and every word of the Buddha's teaching. This is why Dzogchen is known as the "completion teaching." It includes the foundation as well as the central columns, walls, ceiling, and roof. It is beautifully ornamented and furnished. When we practice Dzogchen we should not and cannot ignore any aspect of the teaching.

The gracious teacher Buddha gave many extraordinary teachings—these teachings are about the true nature and nothing else. His entire teaching is about the way things are. In one of the renowned Mahayana sutras called the *Samadhiraja Sutra*, or the *King of Samadhi Sutra*, the Buddha said that there are two truths—relative and absolute—and that there is no third truth. The two truths are expressions of reality. They are not in opposition; one truth is not more important than the other. They appear as two, but they are in union. The teachings say, "one nature, two aspects." It is like fire and its warmth, or the sun and its rays. It is the same for the two truths—they are inseparable.

The Buddha's teachings in general, and his Mahayana teachings in particular, say that if we want realization, we should cooperate with the nature, and practice the two truths. Relative truth practices are called "skillful means," and absolute truth practices are called "wisdom." In the Vajrayana, these are respectively known as the "creation stage visualization" and "completion stage dissolution." By practicing in this way, we will attain full realization without any sidetracks or detours, without falling into the ditches of extreme, narrow views and skeptical mental states.

What are the skillful means practices? These are practices that increase merit, or positive energy, and include cultivating good thoughts like loving-kindness and compassion as well as putting these into action for others' benefit. As we discussed earlier, in the Mahayana, cultivating good thoughts is called "wishing or aspiring bodhichitta," and putting these into action is called "actualizing bodhichitta." Skillful means practices include contemplating the four boundless thoughts, practicing the six paramitas, and doing prostrations and circumambulation. They also include helping to create monuments to enlightened body, speech, and mind such as statues, thangkas, stupas, and monasteries, as well as participating in public works like building, maintaining, and repairing roads and bridges, and working to alleviate poverty and hunger. All positive activities performed with love and compassion are skillful means practices. All of this is part of Dzogchen meditation and helps bring forth realization.

The wisdom practice is meditating on the absolute state of Dzogchen, which means going beyond conceptions. You can begin with shamatha meditation and then go on to vipashyana, or you can immediately practice the union of shamatha and vipashyana. The main thing is to experience and abide in the absolute state of the true nature of the mind. Rest, relax, and be in the natural state without focus or fixation, without grasping and clinging. Abide in the vast, open nature of the deep blue sky. Let thoughts come and go, grasping nothing. This is the heart of wisdom practice.

As long as dualistic mind is functioning, you must perform the relative and absolute truth practices we just described in order to actualize realization. You also need to practice in formal sessions. As your meditation grows stronger, your experience of relative and absolute truth, as well as your skillful means and wisdom practices, gradually merge into a single, inseparable state. At that time, meditation and postmeditation also begin to merge. Yet even when these signs of progress appear, it is very important to keep up your practices. The final goal is total merging, with no separation. It is only dualistic mind's continual grasping on to thoughts and emotions that stands in the way of the final goal.

Every time you complete a formal practice session, you should always conclude with bodhichitta by dedicating the merit and making strong aspiration prayers. Sincerely wish good things for all living beings, without excluding yourself. You can even dedicate the merit and make aspiration prayers after doing something mundane. Keep the teachings alive in your heart and mind as much as you can, and put them into action. Keep growing. This is an overview of how to practice the two truths in union in order to realize the one true nature.

Now we will apply this understanding to the teachings of Aro Yeshe

Jungne. The great master Aro Yeshe Jungne described how to practice Dzogchen meditation nine different ways. But although he taught nine different ways to practice, there are not nine different views—there is only one view because there is only one true nature. And there is only one result: realization of that nature. Master Patrul Rinpoche tells us that according to the oral teachings of many Dzogchen masters, high capability practitioners experience the view and can maintain it the moment they hear the teachings. In other words, their realization of the unity of relative and absolute truths is immediate. Medium capability Dzogchen practitioners cultivate the view in practice. As their meditation develops, realization dawns and in a short time is stabilized. Lesser capability individuals practice skillful means along with wisdom meditation. They gain realization gradually over time with joyful effort. Although the time and effort required to achieve realization vary among practitioners of the three levels of capability, the result they attain is exactly the same. It is the unity of the two truths.

Here Patrul Rinpoche offers this reminder: when your meditation is scattered and your mind is unstable—when it seems as if you are not progressing—focus on the relative skillful means practices like devotion and bodhichitta. Connect to the lineage, cultivate a good heart, and perform virtuous activities. This will stabilize your mind, reinvigorate your practice, and develop momentum for progress toward ultimate realization.

# 27: Devotion and Courage

When we read the histories of the practice lineage, particularly among the Nyingma and Kagyu, we learn that many practitioners who did not attend monastic colleges or receive much formal instruction attained the highest realization. This realization came as a result of their incredible devotion and bodhichitta.

In Buddhism, particularly in the Vajrayana, devotion is very important. With devotion, you appreciate and respect the lineage masters and their teachings, and you stop doubting, hesitating, and searching. Your mind becomes firm, rich, and moist like good soil. With devotion, you are content and realize that everything you have is very precious. Your beautiful qualities bloom, and you see the beautiful qualities in others more vividly than before. You settle into your true nature. Devotion does all this. This is why the Buddha repeatedly said in the tantras that true realization is born from devotion combined with bodhichitta. There is no other method.

Milarepa is renowned in Tibet and also in the West. He was one of the great masters and realized beings, not only in Buddhist history, but in world history as well. After Milarepa met his teacher Marpa, he went through incredible hardship, but the hardship made him stronger. His courage and commitment grew, and his desire to attain liberation intensified. Each and every situation, no matter how difficult, strengthened his devotion. When we read his life story, how much did Marpa give him in the way of formal teachings? In modern times lamas seem to be giving initiations constantly—how many initiations did Milarepa get? Yet because of his faith and trust in Marpa, and his unfailing determination, the external challenges and difficulties Milarepa faced caused him to find everything he was looking for. He put it all into practice, and this is why Milarepa became one of the greatest yogis in history.

The importance of devotion is emphasized not only in the Vajrayana but throughout the Buddha's teachings. The Vinaya—renowned as the foundation teaching of the Buddha—talks about devotion. Examine any Mahayana sutra and you'll read about the importance of devotion. Read the Prajnaparamita teachings in the one hundred thousand-, twenty thousand-, or eight thousand-stanza versions—devotion is stressed throughout. The life story of the Buddha himself is a testament to devotion. The Buddha's realization did not just come by itself. No one handed it to him; it was the fruit of his devotion. This is why the Buddha said that if you do not open the door of devotion, the light of realization will not shine. In the Mahayana sutra called *Light of the Three Jewels*, the Buddha said that devotion is like a hand that gathers every good quality, without which we cannot gather and hold what is good. He also said that devotion is like feet, without which we cannot walk the path to enlightenment.

Here the great master Patrul Rinpoche says that devotion is supported and strengthened by courage. He uses the word *nying-ru*, which is a Tibetan metaphor for courage that means "bone in the heart." In Kagyu prayers, practitioners supplicate the buddhas and lineage masters to develop this quality, saying, "Please bless me to have the bone in my heart." Why is this quality so important? With courage, we are steadfast. Samsara is a habit, and it is always difficult to break habits. Even if our habits cause us suffering, they are familiar and comfortable. Yet with courage, we will not give in to samsara, no matter how enticing it seems—we will break our habits.

Even when we are determined it is not always easy. As samsara crumbles, our minds open and all kinds of thoughts and emotions burst out, some of which are quite ferocious. With courage—the bone in our heart—we will not give in to these thoughts and emotions. We will let them go. Dedicated practitioners always encounter obstacles, not only in terms of thoughts and emotions, but externally as well. We see this in the life story of the wisdom dakini Yeshe Tsogyal. And external obstacles are not always frightening—some are extremely pleasant and inviting. But when we have courage, nothing deters us; we keep moving forward until we reach our final goal.

The Aro teaching says that even if you receive the most powerful teaching in the world, if you do not practice it so that it touches your heart, what good is it? There is a Tibetan expression, "Do not leave the teaching on the pages of a book." We must practice the teachings we receive. If we do not apply the instructions, the strength of the teaching fades away. It's as if we never received it. Activate your joyful effort with appreciation, bodhichitta, devotion, and courage. Practice, and do not stop practicing.

When you do this, the teaching will take root in your heart, where it will blossom and grow, and before too long you and the teaching will become one. On the other hand, if you do not practice the teachings but only say, "I received this teaching, and I received that teaching," you are just telling stories. Reciting a long list of teachings you received but never practiced will not help you when your consciousness departs your body at the time of death. This is why you should take care of your practice right now.

# 28: Beautiful Tips

At this point, Patrul Rinpoche quotes the great Drukpa Kagyu master Götsangpa once again. Based on his own experience, Götsangpa gave six pieces of advice about retreat practice that are useful to practitioners on all levels:

1. The external retreat is to stay in the hermitage.
2. The internal retreat is to sit in your hut or cave.
3. The secret retreat is to sit on your cushion.
4. The most secret retreat is to abide in the nondual state of mind, beyond conceptions, which is the Dzogchen state.
5. Maintain that state without distractions by using mindfulness as a support.
6. Stabilize your conduct by being without attachment and craving.

Patrul Rinpoche continues by saying that there are two ways meditation develops. The first way is that you have to grab meditation. The second way is that meditation grabs you. In the beginning, you have to grab meditation because your mind is not stable. To grab meditation you need mindfulness. Mindfulness is also important when you are intellectually analyzing the view and when you are performing beneficial activities in the world. It is a special wisdom that guides and supports you in all the activities of your life. In particular, when you apply mindfulness to meditation, it means you do not allow yourself to be distracted from the view.

If you keep grabbing meditation in this way, you will gradually discover that meditation is grabbing you. This means that meditation is becoming increasingly natural and effortless. Before too long, you will find that you are always in the meditation state. At that point, whatever comes and goes is part of the display of the true nature. You will no longer distinguish between meditation and nonmeditation.

When meditation grabs you, every thought becomes meditation. How does this happen? When a thought comes and you do not grasp and cling to it, it dissolves. This means that thoughts continue to occur, but since there is freedom from grasping and clinging, they self-liberate and do not disturb you. It is said, "Even if the meditator lets go of meditation, meditation does not let go of the meditator." You have become the meditation.

To reach this stage, practice the view continually with mindfulness. If you practice only occasionally, or if you allow yourself to be distracted, whatever experience you gain through meditation will not last. The teachings refer to this as "rainbow experience." Rainbows appear only for a short time, and once they're gone they leave no trace.

Here Patrul Rinpoche reminds us of the importance of bodhichitta. He says that at the beginning of every session you should reactivate your commitment to benefit all sentient beings, and at the end of the session, you should dedicate the merit, distributing the positive energy of your practice to everyone, everywhere. Use mindfulness to remind yourself to continually deepen and expand your great compassion.

To drive this point home, Patrul Rinpoche quotes the Great Orgyen, Guru Padmasambhava, who said, "Without compassion the root of Dharma practice is rotten." If you somehow ignore compassion, even if you experience signs of progress in your Dzogchen meditation, your practice will become fragile, will wither, and could even die. Therefore, in the beginning generate compassion, in the middle meditate on the absolute truth of the Dzogchen state, and in the end dedicate the merit. Practice like this in many short sessions with great joyful effort.

If you have all these beautiful components, and your meditation is still not as strong as you would like, don't force yourself too much. Take a break and relax. Do other meritorious activities, and then return to meditation. If you keep practicing like this, with a gentle and balanced discipline, your meditation will become increasingly strong and stable. Eventually, the length of time you can abide in the absolute state during the daytime and while you are sleeping will become equal. You will naturally and continuously remain in the natural state. This is called "the full circle of day and night." At that point you can be sure that meditation is grabbing you! In Dzogchen this is called the "supreme state," or *namja chenpo*. In Mahamudra it is called the stage of "nonmeditation."

Remember that at any time, different experiences can arise, such as visions. Do not be distracted. No matter what happens, until your realization is very stable, continue to cultivate bodhichitta, devotion, joyful effort, courage, and commitment, along with your Dzogchen meditation. Keep practicing the union of the two truths.

## Questions and Answers

*At what stage in your practice are you ready for a one- or two-month Dzogchen retreat?*

This depends a lot on your schedule and how much time you can make for retreat. According to the teachings, once you finish ngöndro and have accomplished some degree of the Three Roots accumulation practice, you can focus more on Dzogchen. Of course, even when you are focusing on Dzogchen, at the beginning of each practice session do some chanting to invoke the blessings of the lineage masters, strengthen your compassion, and after meditating, dedicate the merit. Also, do not forget the three hermitage qualities we talked about earlier. If you maintain them, you are always on retreat, even if you are still in the city.

*What is the meaning of the name of the Kagyu master you mentioned earlier, Götsangpa? Could you tell us a little about him?*

*Gö* means "vulture" and *tsang* means "nest." Götsangpa meditated close to a vulture's nest, in a cave in some rocky mountains. For this reason people later named him Götsangpa. He also meditated throughout India, as well as in Oddiyana and other places. His teacher was Tsangpa Gyare, who was also one of the great masters of the Drukpa Kagyu lineage. The histories say that the moment Götsangpa saw Tsangpa Gyare, he felt that he had received everything. He saw his teacher as the Buddha. His devotion was so powerful that he even saw all his teacher's belongings as the Buddha too! Götsangpa attained the highest possible realization.

*Having received so many teachings and empowerments, how can we possibly practice them all?*

Yes, we have received many teachings and empowerments. Now we must synthesize and condense everything, and practice the essence. To do this, begin every practice by cultivating loving-kindness and compassion for all sentient beings. In the Vajrayana, when you visualize the deity and chant mantras, you also cultivate what are known as the "three vajras": realization of the complete purity and perfection of the entire universe as wisdom body, wisdom speech, and wisdom mind. Realize that compassion, the three vajras, deity, and mantra are all empty. Then dedicate the merit. This is the essence of every practice.

*Are the four boundless thoughts connected to the five wisdoms?*

They are not different. With boundless love you are free from anger; freedom from anger is mirrorlike wisdom. With boundless compassion you are free from greed and attachment; freedom from greed and attachment is discriminating wisdom. With boundless joy you are free from jealousy; freedom from jealousy is all-accomplishing wisdom. And with boundless equanimity you are free from arrogance; freedom from arrogance is equanimity wisdom. The fifth wisdom is dharmadhatu wisdom, which is freedom from dualistic conceptions and ignorance. Dharmadhatu wisdom is the essence of the other four wisdoms. This is a brief explanation of how the four boundless thoughts are connected to the five wisdoms according to the teachings of Longchenpa.

*How are the four boundless thoughts and the five wisdoms connected with the three kayas?*

First of all, what is dharmakaya? It is the nature of the mind, beyond duality and ignorance. It is infinite, pure emptiness. So dharmakaya corresponds to dharmadhatu wisdom. The four boundless thoughts of love, compassion, joy, and equanimity, as well as the other four wisdoms, are the expressive energy of the nature of the mind. When these manifest, they appear in sambhogakaya and nirmanakaya forms. The great master Longchenpa made these connections, which are not explained in general Buddhist philosophy. What he is saying is more related to the Dzogchen teachings.

*How is joy connected with the sambhogakaya?*

Joy corresponds to all-accomplishing wisdom, which manifests as the sambhogakaya buddha Amoghasiddhi. The teachings generally say that joy, as well as love, compassion, and equanimity, are manifestations of the clarity aspect of the mind and are therefore part of the sambhogakaya and nirmanakaya. There are many ways to explore and describe this topic—the Buddha's teachings are so profound and deep. As we mentioned, we are relying on the great master Longchenpa for these particular descriptions. But in essence we are talking about special qualities of awakened mind that reflect outwardly to benefit sentient beings. All these special qualities have their source in the dharmakaya and svabhavikakaya. *Dharmakaya* literally means "dharma body," and *svabhavikakaya* means "natural body." It is also called *dharmatakaya*, which means "nature of dharma body." These different names refer to the same thing.

*I notice that when I'm trying not to hold on to thought, I'm subtly rejecting thought.*

Rejecting thought means not wanting it. No matter how subtle this rejection may be, it is still a form of clinging and it creates tension. The teachings always say, "Do not accept and do not reject." Just relax in the natural state, and let thoughts come and go, free from accepting and rejecting. The natural state is also known as the "single-instant state." What is the duration of a single instant? The teachings give many explanations of this. If you pile three hundred and sixty lotus petals on top of one another, a single instant is the time it would take you to press down and pierce all of those petals with a needle. Of course, this example is only for the purposes of giving the conceptual mind something to hold. The Dzogchen teachings say that the single-instant state is actually beyond the three times and beyond measurement.

*I do several practices. How can I merge them into one bodhichitta practice?*

One way is to meditate on Chenrezig, or Avalokiteshvara. Chenrezig is renowned as the embodiment of all the buddhas' love and compassion. As you begin your practice, generate love and compassion for all sentient beings. If you are following a sadhana, visualize Chenrezig and chant the prayers and mantra according to the instructions. All bodhichitta practices are included in the practice of Chenrezig.

Another way is to meditate on any buddha with whom you feel particularly connected. For example, Guru Padmasambhava, Buddha Shakyamuni, and Tara are all embodiments of boundless love and compassion. All the bodhichitta practices are included when you practice on any one of them.

*I am new to Tibetan Buddhism, which has so many techniques and practices. In my homeland, China, we have the Guanyin school, which focuses on devotion to the Goddess of Compassion; she is very similar to Chenrezig. We have Zen, which is simple—in some ways it's like Dzogchen. The Buddha gave so many teachings, and it's impossible to study and meditate on all of them. It seems, however, that all these teachings are designed to remove the* kleshas. *Can you say a little more about this?*

It is true. All the teachings of the Buddha have a single purpose: to remove the kleshas. *Klesha* is a Sanskrit word that means "obscurations." Removing obscurations and revealing buddha-nature is the whole purpose of the Buddha's teaching. There are different techniques to remove obscurations, and different ways of understanding the nature of nirvana—that's why there are many schools. But every Buddhist school agrees that there are obscurations, that they have to be removed, and that there are effective practices which will do just that. It is also agreed that a clear intellectual understanding of the teachings is necessary. The teachings bring realization gradually, swiftly, or instantaneously, depending on the students' capacities and dispositions. The Buddha was like a master chef who cooked and laid out a vast banquet of delicious food. We can choose what we like to fill our tummies.

Meditation is considered by many schools to be the single most essential practice. But many masters achieved enlightenment simply by chanting mantras like OM MANI PEME HUNG or OM AMI DEWA HRI. There are many ways to become realized, and anyone can do this. For example, there is a famous story in the Vinaya about one of the Buddha's disciples who was so slow that he could not even pronounce the four noble truths. Every community thought he was incapable of learning and they rejected him. But through his omniscience, the Buddha saw the potential in this disciple and one day asked him, "What do you know how to do?" The disciple replied, "I don't know how to do anything." Buddha said, "Do you know how to clean the temple?" The disciple replied, "Yes, that I know." So the Buddha said, "Why don't you clean the temple?" The Vinaya teaching says that by cleaning the temple for a while the disciple's mind became more stable. Then the Buddha taught him a few words: "I am cleaning attachment, I am cleaning anger, I am cleaning ignorance." The disciple started to chant these words as he cleaned. At first he did not understand what he was chanting, but in time he began to wonder, "What is attachment, anger, and ignorance?" He began to realize that these were not outside himself, but within, and they were negative qualities that should be removed. He started cleaning and chanting at the same time, and he practiced this way with great joyful effort. In time, all his obscurations were removed. He attained realization and became one of the sixteen arhats. This great teacher's name was Lamtren Tan. His portrait is painted in the temple murals at Padma Samye Ling.

# 29: A Brief History of Dzogchen

WHO FIRST TAUGHT Dzogchen? The Dzogchen histories speak of twelve Dzogchen buddhas. Among these, Buddha Shakyamuni is the twelfth. Since Buddha Shakyamuni appeared almost 2,600 years ago, and the eleven other Dzogchen buddhas came before him, it means the Dzogchen lineage is extremely ancient.

But the Dzogchen teaching did not begin and end with these twelve buddhas. The Dzogchen teaching is beyond beginning and ending; it is the indestructible, continuous proclamation of the true nature. The true nature is fully awakened intelligence, which is known as Buddha Samantabhadra, the All-Good Buddha.

Every sentient being has inherited this fully awakened intelligence, and every sentient being, without exception, has the right and the opportunity to realize it. Dzogchen is the reminder for us to awaken, the means to do so, and the awakened state itself. In the *Manjushri-nama-samgiti Tantra*, *Chanting the Names of Manjushri*, it says that the Dzogchen teaching has echoed in the past, echoes in the present, and will continue to echo in the future. Dzogchen simultaneously encompasses and transcends the three times.

Buddha Samantabhadra manifested as all twelve of the Dzogchen buddhas. Each of these buddhas appeared in a particular way and taught specific teachings that were appropriate for the beings of their time. In our world, at this time, Buddha Samantabhadra emanated as Buddha Shakyamuni. The Buddha did not give Dzogchen teachings publicly. He taught Dzogchen privately to select individuals who had the capacity to understand it. Most of all, he taught Dzogchen to beings in the higher realms.

About thirty years after the Buddha's mahaparinirvana, a remarkable emanation being named Garab Dorje took birth west of India. Even though he was already enlightened, he sought out both human and nonhuman teachers, and practiced and meditated in order to show the way to others. He also gathered the Dzogchen teachings that Buddha Shakyamuni taught in the higher realms. Afterward, Garab Dorje transmitted the complete Dzogchen teachings to only one person: his principal disciple, Manjushrimitra. Manjushrimitra gave the complete teachings, once more as a single lineage, to Shri Singha. Garab Dorje, Manjushrimitra, and Shri Singha all accomplished the transcendental wisdom rainbow body. Shri Singha was the first of the great Dzogchen masters to transmit the complete teachings more widely. He gave them first to his three principal disciples—Jnanasutra, Vimalamitra, and Guru Padmasambhava—and then later in his wisdom body to the great Tibetan translator Vairochana.

In the eighth century Buddhism became fully established in Tibet, largely due to the powerful aspirations and effort of King Trisong Deutsen. At that time, Tibet was the most powerful nation in central Asia, and King Trisong Deutsen wanted to bring everlasting peace and happiness to his subjects and to all the neighboring lands. He observed that many of the surrounding countries were practicing the Dharma, and he began to seriously study the Dharma. He was inspired by the teachings of the Buddha on love, compassion, nonviolence, and discovering the true nature. He thought, "This message is so profound. I want to bring this teaching to Tibet, and leave a legacy that will benefit my country for a long time." King Trisong Deutsen took action by inviting the great masters Shantarakshita and Guru Padmasambhava to Tibet. Together they built the great Samye monastery and inaugurated a vast translation project. Later King Trisong Deutsen invited other great masters to Tibet who came mostly from India but also from other countries along the Silk Road, as well as from Sri Lanka and China. These masters and their Tibetan students collected, translated, and edited the complete teachings of the Buddha, including the Hinayana, Mahayana, and Vajrayana. The work of these masters was not only scholastic—they taught meditation as well. In particular, Guru Padmasambhava gave Dzogchen teachings. Many dedicated Tibetans practiced these teachings and attained realization within a single lifetime. All of this occurred during the eighth century and in the beginning of the ninth; it was the golden age of Dharma in Tibet.

Once the Mahayana teachings were translated and established, Guru Padmasambhava and Shantarakshita urged King Trisong Deutsen to invite the great master Vimalamitra to Tibet in order to further glorify the Dzogchen teachings. Vimalamitra was one of the great scholars at that time, and on the realization level he had achieved the transcendental wisdom rainbow body. He came to Tibet and gave extensive teachings, particularly on Dzogchen. Guru Padmasambhava and Shantarakshita also encouraged a number of young Tibetan scholar-meditators to go to India and observe how the teachings were taught and practiced in the birthplace of Buddhism. They did this so that King Trisong Deutsen and other Tibetans would feel confident that the Dharma they received was pure and authentic. The king arranged everything, and sent Vairochana and other translators to India. When they returned to Tibet, Vairochana and the other translators affirmed that the Dharma taught by Guru Padmasambhava and Shantarakshita was the same Dharma that was taught in India.

Now we will say a few words about the great master Vairochana. Vairochana was one of the principal disciples of Guru Padmasambhava and Shantarakshita. He was renowned as the reincarnation of the Buddha's chief disciple, Ananda, and also as an emanation of Buddha Vairochana. Vairochana was a highly realized being even before he went to India. Once in India, he sought out many masters; in particular, he met and received Dzogchen teachings from the wisdom body of the great master Shri Singha. Vairochana returned to Tibet with many great teachings, including some important Dzogchen texts. Then, under the guidance of Guru Padmasambhava, Shantarakshita, and Vimalamitra, he translated and edited them.

Vairochana became one of the first and greatest native Tibetan teachers. Guru Padmasambhava and Vimalamitra honored him, praising his knowledge and realization. Later Vairochana traveled to eastern Tibet near the Chinese border, to the land of Gyarong. He stayed there a long time, giving extensive Dzogchen instructions as well as other teachings. Many of his students attained enlightenment.

As we said, this was a golden age for the Dharma in Tibet. Countless practitioners achieved the highest realization. Renowned among them were Guru Padmasambhava's students, such as King Trisong Deutsen and the twenty-five disciples, the eighty mahasiddhas of the Yerpa region, the hundred and eight great meditators at Mt. Chiwo, the thirty-five dakinis, and the seven yoginis. Through the practice of Dzogchen, many of these practitioners achieved the transcendental wisdom rainbow body. Dzogchen became popular—lineages developed and spread throughout Tibet and into surrounding countries. Many of these lineages continue to thrive even now, and of course many have come to the West. From the time of Guru Padmasambhava through the present day, the practice of Dzogchen has been renowned for the speed and power with which it propels devoted practitioners to the ultimate goal of spiritual life.

# 30: Concluding Words: Bodhichitta Is the Core

Dzogchen practitioners must combine their meditation on emptiness with compassion. Emptiness means egolessness. This means freedom from selfishness and all clinging. Compassion means caring for all sentient beings and helping them find total peace and happiness. Practicing on emptiness alone will not help you reach enlightenment. There is a non-Buddhist meditation school in India that teaches that the realization of emptiness comes from completely blocking all sensory experiences. Even if this practice leads to emptiness-realization, if you have trained yourself in blocking the senses how can you practice compassion? It is not our intention to promote Buddhism and devalue other schools. We just want to remind you that the true nature of the mind is the unity of emptiness and compassion.

The Dzogchen teachings always talk about emptiness and clarity. Emptiness refers to the utter openness of the nature of the mind, while clarity refers to the rich and beautiful qualities inherent in the nature of the mind. Compassion is one of these qualities. If we accept emptiness and reject compassion, we're knocking our heads against a wall. Therefore, don't be partial—be open to the fullness of the teachings and the fullness of yourself. All the great teachers have said this. We must practice the unity of emptiness and compassion, wisdom and skillful means, absolute truth and relative truth. When we do this, realization comes beautifully and perfectly.

Buddha Shakyamuni once gave an important teaching to the king of Kosala in his capital city of Shravasti. This is where the Buddha taught the *Diamond Sutra*. Addressing the king of Kosala, the Buddha said, "Oh great king, you perform many activities, and do not have much time for spiritual pursuits, but if you keep one thing in your heart, you are practicing the Dharma—that is bodhichitta." Bodhichitta is the core of the Buddha's teachings, and the core of Guru Padmasambhava's teachings. It is the essential teaching of all the great masters who followed them.

Tibet is renowned as one of the world's great spiritual countries because of its teachings and practice of compassion. When there has been trouble in Tibet, the teachings of the Buddha and Guru Padmasambhava have prevented conditions from becoming worse. When we read political and religious histories that span many centuries, we see that although Tibet has not been perfect, it has done quite well compared to other countries. In recent times, ego-clinging and negative emotions have manifested wildly, and Tibet has been overrun by a foreign invader. But the Tibetan people and their culture have endured. This is due to the Dharma, and compassion.

Please keep this in your heart and mind as we review the practice one more time. At the beginning of each meditation session, generate bodhichitta for all beings. Reflect on impermanence. Feel the presence of Guru Padmasambhava, and all the buddhas, bodhisattvas, lineage masters, and sangha. Chant the seven-line prayer, which is the sound of love, joy, and devotion. Feel the sacred sound of this prayer purifying all emotional turbulence and ego-clinging. Feel it bringing you and all beings back into your original true nature. If you recite any additional prayers and mantras, continue generating these beautiful thoughts. Whether you recite for a short or long time, afterward meditate on the absolute state—open, relaxed, and free. Meditate according to your capabilities, beginning with focus for a while if you need it, then ultimately relaxing without any focus according to the Dzogchen teachings. Even when your meditation is going well, from time to time rekindle positive thoughts, as it is recommended in the Aro teachings. When your meditation is not going well, again use the assistance of skillful means—revitalize yourself by invoking joy, appreciation, love, and devotion, and return to Dzogchen meditation. At the conclusion of the session, dedicate the merit for all living beings.

During the day, maintain good thoughts as much as you can. Cultivate patience, tolerance, and forgiveness—this will prevent negative emotions from overwhelming you. Help others according to your abilities and their needs. At night when you go to bed, invoke the blessings of the enlightened beings, reactivate your motivation, and do your dream yoga practice. This is a brief summary of the teachings. By practicing in this way, realization will come.

And here we conclude with the words of Aro Yeshe Jungne, "AH, AH, AH."

Bodhichitta Is the Core of the Buddha's Teachings

# Dedication of Merit

May the victory banner of the fearless teachings of the Ancient Tradition be raised.
May the victorious drum of the teaching and practice of Dharma resound in the ten directions.
May the lion's roar of reasoning pervade the three places.
May the light of unequaled virtues increase.

May all the temples and monasteries,
All the readings and recitations of the Dharma flourish.
May the sangha always be in harmony,
And may their aspirations be achieved.

At this very moment, for the peoples and nations of the earth,
May not even the names of disease, famine, war, and suffering be heard.
But rather may pure conduct, merit, wealth, and prosperity increase,
And may supreme good fortune and well-being always arise.

# Notes

1. *Theg mchog a ti'i man ngag gnas lugs gsal ston,* including *Gzhan yang zhal shes 'thor bu.* In *The Collected Works of Dpal-sprul O-rgyan-'jigs-med-chos-kyi-dbang-po* (Gangtok: Sonam T. Kazi, 1970–71). TBRC W5832. Vol. 4 (*nga*), pp. 709–35.
2. A burned-up rope still has the appearance of a rope when the ashes stick together, but as soon as one attempts to use it, the ashes disintegrate because there is no pith or essence to them. (This and all comments are based on oral commentary by Khenchen Palden Sherab Rinpoche, henceforth KPSR.)
3. The Great Orgyen (O rgyan chen po) is one name for Padmasambhava, or Guru Rinpoche, the great master from Orgyen (Skt. Uḍḍiyāna), the crucial figure in bringing Buddhism to Tibet.
4. Mitrayogin (Mi tra dzo ki or Mi pham sbas pa'i bshes gnyen), a mahasiddha from Radha in Orissa, eastern India, who later came to Tibet (George N. Roerich, *The Blue Annals* [Delhi: Motilal Banarsidass, 1976], pp. 1030–43).
5. Zhijé (Tib. *zhi byed*), a lineage of teachings originating with Pa Dampa Sangye (ca. eleventh–twelfth centuries).
6. Gyalwa Yangönpa, also known as Gyaltsenpal (rGyal ba Yang dgon pa / rGyal mtshan dpal; 1213–1258, alt. 1153–1198), the primary disciple of Götsangpa and one of the main masters of the Upper Drukpa Kagyu lineage and its subsect, the Bara Kagyu.
7. The five eyes or five levels of clairvoyant vision (Tib. *spyan lnga*) are the physical eye, the divine eye, the eye of knowledge, the dharma eye, and the buddha eye (*sha'i spyan, lha'i spyan, shes rab kyi spyan, chos kyi spyan, sangs rgyas kyi spyan*).
8. Clairvoyance or superknowledge or actual knowing (Tib. *mngon shes*) refers to the six superknowledges: the capacities for performing miracles, divine sight, divine hearing, recollection of former lives, cognition of the minds of others, and the cognition of the exhaustion of defilements.
9. The four meditative concentration states (Tib. *bsam gtan bzhi*; Skt. *dhyāna*): (1) joy and reflection; (2) joy and absence of reflection; (3) being free of joy, and equable concentration states; (4) supreme equanimity.
10. Four spheres of perception (Tib. *skye mched mu bzhi*) refers to the mind states

or absorptions that constitute the four formless realms: Infinite Space, Infinite Consciousness, Nothing Whatsoever, and Neither Presence nor Absence of Conception. Also called the immaterial states.

11. Usually, the nine concentrations of equilibrium (Tib. *snyoms 'jug gi bsam gtan dgu*). These are the four concentrations, the four formless states, and the shravaka's absorption of peace. KPSR adds that it is best to call them the *'gog pa'i snyoms par 'jug pa dgu*, "the nine equilibriums of cessation."
12. "Heretics" (Tib. *mu stegs pa*; Skt. *tīrthika*) refers to teachers of non-Buddhist philosophy who adhere to the extreme views of eternalism or nihilism.
13. Khenchen Palden Sherab's definition of superior insight (Tib. *lhag mthong*; Skt. *vipaśyanā*) is interesting here: *lhag* means "special" and *mthong* means "seeing," and what is seen is nonself. The heretics strive to realize the great self (Skt. *brahmā*) or the individual self (Skt. *ātman*), but essentially this is not different from ordinary people, since everybody normally has a sense or perception of a self. Therefore it is not special (*lhag*). Only Buddhists see nonself, and therefore it is special or superior insight (*lhag mthong*).
14. Gyalwa Götsangpa Gönpo Dorje (rGyal ba rGod tshang pa mgon po rdo rje), 1189–1258. Götsangpa (literally, "Vulture Nest Dweller") was a great master in the Drukpa Kagyu lineage and was named after a cave where he did intensive practice.
15. Freedom from embellishment (Tib. *spros bral*) refers to the second of the four levels or yogas of Mahamudra (Tib. *phyag rgya chen po'i rnal 'byor bzhi*): one-pointed (*rtse gcig*), unembellished (*spros bral*), single flavor (*ro gcig*), and nonmeditation (*sgom med*).
16. In other words, cannot believe in emptiness. (KPSR)
17. "A lack of thought similar to nonthought" (Tib. *rnam rtog med pa'i mi rtog pa 'dra mo*) is explained as a dull or dark unconscious state without thought (*rnam rtog med pa*), similar to but not the genuine meditative experience of nonthought (*mi rtog pa'i nyams*) that is the result of effective calm abiding practice.
18. The lesser undivided attention (Tib. *rtse gcig chung ngu*) is the lesser of the three phases (lesser, middle, and greater) of the first level or yoga, called one-pointed or undivided, in the Mahamudra tradition. See note 15.
19. The absorption of a hearer (Tib. *nyan thos 'gogs pa'i [ting nge 'dzin]*). Of the stages of samadhi or meditative absorption, this state of the cessation of all sensation (*tshor ba med pa*) or conceptualization (*'du shes med pa*) is considered the highest for a hearer (Skt. *śrāvaka*). Here, however, in the explanation of superior insight in the Mahamudra and Dzogchen perspectives, it is seen as a possible trap.
20. These five meditative experiences of absorption (Tib. *ting nge 'dzin nyams lnga*) are also called, respectively, wavering (*g.yo*), attainment (*thob*), familiarization (*goms*), stability (*brtan*), and consummation (*mthar phyin*).
21. Milarepa (1040–1123), the great yogin of the Kagyu lineage, was showing his disciple, the monk Gampopa (1079–1153), that his accomplishment of the four absorptions was no big deal without intelligence (Skt. *prajñā*), since they were commonly achieved even by non-Buddhists.

22. Khenchen Palden Sherab comments: In early times when ships sailed the seas, there were sea-monsters (Tib. *chu zin*). Sailors were scared and uncertain. So they sent a crow or a pigeon off. There was no land around, so if the bird did not return, it meant that it had landed on the sea-monster's head. If it returned, all was clear.
23. "To take hold" (Tib. *phar 'jus*) and "to be held" (*tshur 'jus*): the first is in the beginning, since the mind is so perturbed, thinking that you need to meditate, calm the mind, and so on—in other words, making meditation a distinct object (*bzung ba*). The latter is when the essential empty nature of thoughts is automatically seen, and then meditation is natural and inseparable, not the object, but rather the subject itself (*'dzin pa*). (KPSR)
24. "The mind that is not ready" (Tib. *las su ma rung*) refers to the mind that is not independent, a person who has no control or ownership of their own mind (*bdag po kyab ma thub pa*). (KPSR)
25. "Held by meditation" (Tib. *tshur 'jus*): see note 23. "Around the clock" (*'khor yug ma*) means that mindfulness is naturally present during dream states and so on, thus totally integrated as inseparable, or "to be held."
26. No meditation (Tib. *sgom med*), the fourth of the four levels of Mahamudra. See note 15.
27. That is, it is called a view, although it is a meditation, because it still maintains some degree of mental examination. (KPSR)
28. Chos rje 'Ba' ra ba rGyal mtshan dpal bzang (1310–1391), founder of the Bara Kagyu, a subsect of Drukpa Kagyu.
29. Tib. *bzod pa*, in this case referring to the meditative stage of forbearance on the path of application.
30. The following is a brief commentary on the famous teaching attributed to Garab Dorje called "Three Words That Strike the Crucial Point" (*Tshig gsum gnad brdegs*). Patrul Rinpoche himself wrote a well-known commentary on this, called *The Special Teaching of the Wise and Glorious Sovereign* (*Mkhas pa sri rgyal po'i khyad chos*). See *The Lion's Gaze* (Sky Dancer Press, 1998) for a translation by Sarah Harding with commentary by Khenchen Palden Sherab and Khenpo Tsewang Dongyal.
31. Mind (Tib. *sems*) refers to dualistic conceptuality. Mind-as-such (*sems nyid*) refers to the true being (Tib. *chos nyid*; Skt. *dharmatā*, or "dharmaness") of mind, the emptiness. (KPSR)
32. Because you are always abiding within dharmata. (KPSR)
33. The three unmoving states (Tib. *mi 'gul ba gsum*) are (1) without moving from the postures of the body, the energy channels and currents are relaxed of their own accord; (2) without moving from the gazes of the eyes, appearances are enhanced; and (3) without moving from the state of the unfabricating mind, the expanse and awareness are integrated.
34. The threefold "freely resting" (Tib. *cog bzhag gsum*) is usually enumerated as (1) freely resting mountain (*ri bo cog bzhag*), (2) freely resting ocean (*rgya mtsho cog bzhag*), and (3) freely resting awareness (*rig pa cog bzhag*).

# Glossary

***Abhidharma*** is the third of the Three Baskets of the Buddha's teachings, the other two being the Vinaya and Sutras. The Abhidharma includes teachings on Buddhist psychology and logic, descriptions of the universe, the steps on the path to enlightenment, descriptions of the different kinds of beings, and refutations of mistaken beliefs.

***Absolute truth*** refers to the ultimate nature of the mind and the true nature of all phenomena, the state beyond all conceptual constructs, and beyond arising, dwelling, and ceasing.

***Akanishtha*** literally means "what is not below." It is the highest of the pure lands—one's own mind free of concepts and emotions.

***Amoghasiddhi*** is the buddha who personifies the transformation of jealousy into joy and the all-accomplishing wisdom. He also represents the essence of the wind element.

***Anuyoga*** is the second of the three inner tantras according to the nine-yana system of the Nyingma school of Tibetan Buddhism. According to Anuyoga, the view to be realized is that all things are enlightened from the very beginning. Practitioners of Anuyoga assert that the mind's nature free from conceptual constructs is a limitlessly spacious readiness to respond, its brightness without objectification is primordial wisdom, and their nonduality is great bliss. The path of Anuyoga comprises both common and extraordinary components, the latter of which include the definitive path of skillful means and the liberating path of discriminating awareness. The definitive path of skillful means includes practices based on the hidden structure of our inherent vajra body. See also ***nine yanas***.

***Arhat*** literally means "foe-destroyer." This term refers to beings who have conquered their "enemies"—the afflictive emotions—by realizing the nonsubstantiality of the self. By doing so they are freed from suffering, but they do not achieve complete buddhahood until they realize the nonsubstantiality of all phenomena.

***Asuras*** are a class of beings called demigods who are always fighting and jealously scheming on how to overcome the gods.

***Atisha*** (982–1054) was a revered teacher of Buddhism in India who became prominent as the abbot of Vikramashila monastic university. Invited to Tibet, he spent the last seventeen years of his life teaching and traveling in that country, and it was there that his famous *Lamp for the Path to Enlightenment* was composed.

*Atiyoga* is the third of the three inner tantras, the first two being Mahayoga and Anuyoga. According to Jamgon Kongtrul, it emphasizes the method of growing accustomed to the recognition of the nature of the mind, which is free from hope and fear, acceptance and rejection. *Atiyoga* is a synonym for Dzogchen, also translated as Great Perfection and Great Completion. *Ati* means "supreme."

*Avalokiteshvara* is the Buddha of Infinite Compassion. He is also the Lord of Speech.

*Awareness*, when used by masters of Dzogchen, means mind devoid of ignorance and dualistic fixation.

*Bardo* means intermediate state. Khenpo Tsewang Dongyal Rinpoche says that *bardo* is synonymous with "dream." There are generally six bardos enumerated, of which the most commonly referred to is the state between death and the next rebirth. The six bardos are

1. the ground bardo of the natural condition,
2. the meditation bardo of luminosity,
3. the dream bardo of deluded experience,
4. the death bardo of disturbed elements,
5. the dharmata bardo of spontaneous presence, and
6. the karmic bardo of becoming.

*Bodhichitta* literally means the "mind of enlightenment." Relative bodhichitta is the wish to attain buddhahood for the sake of all sentient beings by practicing the path of love, compassion, and wisdom. Absolute bodhichitta recognizes that all beings are primordially enlightened; there is no liberator, no liberated, and no action of liberation since nothing ever moves from the absolute space of the dharmadhatu, or rigpa. Resting in this great immovable space is the ultimate bodhichitta.

*Bodhisattvayana* means "bodhisattva's vehicle." It contains the teachings and practices that enable one to perfect bodhichitta in both its relative and absolute aspects.

A *buddha* is one who has completely awakened from the fundamental ignorance of the two obscurations and developed unceasing pristine cognition of buddha-nature. Having cultivated every positive quality to its utmost limit, buddhas have traversed the bodhisattva levels and eliminated all obscurations to true knowledge. Thus, they enjoy the five fruitional aspects of a buddha's body, speech, mind, qualities, and activities, or the "five wheels of inexhaustible adornment." Buddha Shakyamuni is the buddha of this era, but innumerable buddhas of the past have shown the way to enlightenment, and innumerable buddhas will teach the way to enlightenment in the future.

*Calm abiding*. See *shamatha*.

A *cause* is the motivating power, reason, seed, or basis for an action or a result.

A *chakra* is a focal point of subtle energy within the central channel of the body.

There are five primary chakras: the crown, the throat, the heart, the navel, and the secret chakra. Various practices may work with fewer or more than these.

***Channels*** are the energy pathways of the subtle body, within which the winds and elements move. There are three main channels and thousands of branch channels.

***Clarity*** refers to the power of the mind—its wakeful, knowing, and expressive nature.

A ***condition*** is one of many factors that must be present in order for a cause to produce a particular result. For example, water, soil, and warmth must be present for a period of time in order for a seed to sprout.

***Crazy wisdom*** refers to powerful action—miraculous, unexpected, unconventional, and sometimes even outrageous—that inspires and evokes spiritual awakening in others. Guru Padmasambhava is the quintessence of crazy wisdom. Other great masters of crazy wisdom in Tibetan Buddhist history include Sangye Lingpa, Dudul Dorje, Lhatsun Namkha Jigme, Tsasum Lingpa, Do Khyentse, and Dudjom Lingpa.

***Dharmadhatu*** literally means "the realm of phenomena," which refers to the suchness in which emptiness and dependently arisen mere appearances are inseparable. This is the nature of mind and phenomena—emptiness—that is free from arising, dwelling, and ceasing.

***Dharmakaya*** is the ultimate nature and essence of enlightened mind on the absolute level. On the relative level, it indicates the primordial purity of phenomena, related with the fact that all phenomena are equal in the state of great emptiness. The dharmakaya is uncreated, free from conceptual elaboration, naturally radiant, empty of inherent existence, and spacious like the sky. Although it cannot adequately be expressed in words, the dharmakaya is the emptiness nature that pervades all phenomena.

***Dharmata*** is the intrinsic absolute nature of everything; the true essence of things as they are.

The ***Diamond Sutra*** is a renowned Mahayana text emphasizing the practice of nonabiding and nonattachment.

***Do Khyentse*** (1800–1866) was one of the most amazing masters of miraculous power in Tibetan Buddhist history. He was the mind emanation of Jigme Lingpa, a heart-son of the First Dodrupchen Jigme Thinley Ozer, a terton, and an extraordinary and totally unconventional spiritual guide.

***Duality*** refers to the ordinary perceptual framework of unenlightened beings where mind is seen as "I" and external phenomena are seen as "other." Grasping on to the apparent separation between self and other is the fundamental cause of suffering.

The ***Dudjom Tersar Ngöndro*** is a renowned set of *ngöndro*, or preliminary practices, discovered as termas by the great master Dudjom Lingpa, as well as by his reincarnation, His Holiness Dudjom Rinpoche.

***Dzogchen***, also known as Atiyoga and often translated as "Great Completion" or "Great Perfection," is the highest teaching of Buddha Shakyamuni and the ninth and last vehicle of the Nyingma school of Tibetan Buddhism. In Tibet, it was transmitted through three principal teachers: Guru Padmasambhava, Vimalamitra, and Vairochana. Through the practice of Dzogchen all enlightened attributes are effortlessly perfected in one's own intrinsic, primordial awareness, or rigpa. According to the Dzogchen teachings, the nature of awareness is empty in essence, luminous in nature, and unconfined in capacity; furthermore, these three characteristics are indivisible. According to tradition, one completes ngöndro before moving on the special Dzogchen preliminaries. A practitioner receives the pointing-out instructions from a qualified lama and is thus introduced to the nature of mind, or rigpa. Upon recognizing one's own innate nature and having this confirmed by the guru, one trains in stabilizing this wisdom awareness by recognizing and abiding in mind essence again and again. As explained throughout the teachings, Dzogchen has been transmitted in three lineages: Mind, Space, and Essence Instruction Sections. The Essence Instruction Section effects the stabilization of rigpa awareness by training in the two special methods of trekchö and tögal. See ***nine yanas***.

***Dzogchen Semde***. See ***Mind Section of Dzogchen***.

***Emptiness*** refers to the ultimate nature of both mind and external phenomena. When mind and external phenomena are experienced without intellectual and emotional interference, they are utterly open, free, and beyond conception.

The ***Essence Instruction Section*** of Dzogchen transmission includes the innermost teachings of the Great Perfection in the form of the esoteric pith instructions, as well as the unsurpassed practices of trekchö and tögal. These teachings were taught mainly by Padmasambhava and Vimalamitra.

***Fabrications*** are the stories and fantasies—they can take the form of rules and facts—that we weave about ourselves and our world, based on habitual patterns of thought and emotion.

***Garab Dorje***, a manifestation of Vajrasattva, was the first human teacher of Dzogchen, miraculously born to the virgin daughter of the king of Oddiyana, a land thought by some scholars to be located in what is today known as Swat Valley, Pakistan. It is held that he recited many Dzogchen tantras at the moment of his birth and soon began to transmit these teachings "beyond effort" to worthy students. His last testament, the *Three Statements That Strike the Crucial Point*, was given at the time of his mahaparinirvana to his principal disciple, Manjushrimitra, and is the heart essence of the entire Dzogchen teaching. The "Three Statements" are as follows:

1. Directly introduce the nature of the mind.
2. Decide to abide in the nature of the mind.
3. Gain confidence in liberation.

***Götsangpa*** (1189–1258), a great wandering yogi of the Drukpa Kagyu lineage, was thought by many to be the incarnation of Milarepa. He was renowned for his ability to take obstacles as the path. He completely fulfilled the last teaching that his guru, Tsangpa Gyare, imparted to him: "Give up concerns for the present life. Stay in mountain retreats." It was Götsangpa who charted the route for circumambulating sacred Mt. Kailash.

***Grasping*** refers to the subjectively oriented mental process of taking hold of, apprehending, seizing, or clinging to perceptions. In simple terms, grasping means believing that one's thoughts and emotions are true, and then speaking and acting with this as a foundation.

***Great Completion***, or ***Great Perfection***. See ***Dzogchen***.

***Great Seal***. See ***Mahamudra***.

***Guru Padmasambhava*** is an emanation of Buddha Amitabha and Avalokiteshvara, born miraculously on a lotus in Dhanakosha Lake (sometimes called Sindu Lake) in the land of Oddiyana, northwest of India. He is the embodiment of all the buddhas of the three times and the ten directions, and was predicted by Buddha Shakyamuni as his own reincarnation, who would teach all of the sutras and tantras. He is a buddha who attained the transcendental wisdom rainbow body, an ever-youthful immortal body. In the eighth century, Shantarakshita encouraged King Trisong Deutsen to invite him to Tibet in order to subdue the forces that were thwarting the establishment of the Buddhadharma. Out of compassion for future generations, knowing that the oral transmission lineage of the Buddha's teachings would either become lost or diluted, he hid innumerable Dharma treasures of texts and relics, known as terma, throughout Tibet, Nepal, Bhutan, and elsewhere to be discovered by destined disciples, known as tertons, in the centuries to come. Guru Padmasambhava is a living buddha, ever-present and available, manifesting in infinite forms, who at all times and in all places fulfills the temporal and spiritual wishes of all beings.

The ***Heart Sutra*** is perhaps the most famous of all the Prajnaparamita texts. Its full name is the "Heart of Transcendent Wisdom." The *Heart Sutra* teaches the emptiness of all phenomena.

***Hinayana*** literally means "Lesser Vehicle," since this group of Buddhist teachings focuses on individual enlightenment rather than on that of all sentient beings. The Hinayana comprises the foundational Buddhist teachings that emphasize monastic discipline, strict meditation, contemplation of the four noble truths, renunciation of the worldly distractions of samsara, and rigorous study of the twelve links of dependent origination, all of which eventually bring about the realization of the emptiness of self and thereby liberation from cyclic existence, known as arhathood. Hinayana is the essential foundation of both Mahayana and Vajrayana Buddhism. See ***nine yanas***.

***Impermanence*** is one of the essential points of Buddha Shakyamuni's teaching. There are two forms of impermanence: gross impermanence refers to the obvious constant change perceived by the senses, while subtle impermanence reflects the fact that nothing can remain identical to itself even from one moment to the next.

The ***inner tantras*** include Mahayoga, Anuyoga, and Atiyoga according to the nine-yana system of the Nyingma school. With infinite compassion and confidence in the enlightened nature of everything, one instantly arises as a buddha in an enlightened environment and performs enlightened activities to instantly dispel all suffering caused by mistaken dualistic conceptions and negative emotions. See ***nine yanas***.

***Jigme Gyalwai Nyugu*** (1765–1843), along with the First Dodrupchen Jigme Thinley Ozer, was responsible for the spread of the Longchen Nyingtik lineage throughout Tibet, particularly in the east. When he first met his root teacher, Jigme Lingpa, he felt such profound devotion that immediate realization of the Dzogchen view dawned in his heart. He was an embodiment of Avalokiteshvara, a beloved teacher, and a profound realization being.

***Jigme Lingpa*** (1730–1798) was an emanation of both Vimalamitra and King Trisong Deutsen's grandson, Prince Lhaje. One of the greatest visionaries in Tibetan history, he discovered the Longchen Nyingtik, or the Heart Essence of Longchenpa—which is among the most widely practiced terma cycles—and was also a poet, siddha, and scholar. All his knowledge was gained through Dzogchen meditation rather than through study. He therefore exemplifies the teachings that assert that once the true nature is discovered and stabilized, all wisdom is spontaneously revealed.

***Jnana Kumara***, also known as Nyak Jnana Kumara, was one of the twenty-five disciples of Guru Padmasambhava, as well as a disciple of Shantarakshita and Vimalamitra. He was the first great native-Tibetan lineage holder of the kama teachings, as well as a renowned translator and scholar. Four of his treatises still exist, which are mainly related to the *Guhyagarbha Tantra*, or the *Secret Essence Tantra: The Net of Magical Illusions*. He also translated over forty-four of the inner tantras and their commentaries. Jnana Kumara is usually depicted on thangkas and murals as extracting nectar or water from dry mountain rock.

***Jnanasutra*** was born to a low-caste family in Kamalashila, eastern India. He became a scholar and went to Bodhgaya, where he met Vimalamitra. Vajrasattva appeared in the sky to both of them, saying, "O noble sons, you have been scholars for five hundred lives without having achieved your spiritual goals. If you want to attain enlightenment and the transcendental wisdom rainbow body in this lifetime, you should go receive the Dzogchen teachings from Shri Singha." Vimalamitra went to Shri Singha first, received teachings, and returned. Then Jnanasutra went to Shri Singha and stayed, studying with and serving him for many years. Shri Singha gave Jnanasutra the complete Dzogchen teachings, including those Vimalamitra had not received, as well as his last testament, the *Seven Nails*. Later, Jnanasutra gave all the teachings he received from Shri Singha to Vimalamitra. When Jnanasutra attained the transcendental wisdom rainbow body, he imparted his last testament, the *Four Methods of Contemplation*, to Vimalamitra:

> Homage to the primordially pure emptiness.
> How wonderful! If you train in this, joy will naturally arise.

If you wish to attain the state of great equanimity, gain experience in these contemplations:

1. If you wish to be trained in all esoteric activities, maintain all appearances in the directness of natural contemplation.
2. If you wish to gain strength in your meditation, remain in the unity of mind and phenomena, through the ocean-like natural contemplation.
3. If you wish to attain self-liberation from all views, bring phenomena to cessation through the mountain-like natural contemplation.
4. If you wish to attain all the results as they are, liberate all the errors in training with the mountain-like view.

***Kadam*** was the first of the four New Translation schools of Tibetan Buddhism. It followed the teachings of Atisha and emphasized bodhichitta, intellectual study, and exemplary moral conduct. Although the Kadam no longer exists as a separate tradition, its teachings have influenced and been incorporated into the lineages of all the other schools.

***Kagyu*** means "hearing lineage," and it is one of the four New Translation schools of Tibetan Buddhism. The Kagyu follows the teachings of Tilopa and Naropa, which were brought to Tibet in the eleventh century by Marpa and transmitted to Milarepa.

***Kama*** refers to the oral transmission of the Nyingma school, the body of teachings translated during the period when Guru Padmasambhava was in Tibet, which have been transmitted in an uninterrupted and continuous lineage through to this day.

***King Songtsen Gampo*** (617–695) was an emanation of Avalokiteshvara, unified Tibet for the first time in recorded history and established its dominion as a major central Asian power, and was instrumental in spreading Buddhism throughout the land.

***King Trisong Deutsen*** (742–810), along with Guru Padmasambhava and Shantarakshita, established Buddhism in Tibet. During his reign, Tibet became perhaps the most powerful nation in central Asia. An emanation of Manjushri and a realized being, his reincarnations include the two terton kings, Nyangral Nyima Ozer and Guru Chowang.

The ***Lankavatara Sutra*** is a famous Mahayana text that teaches that all phenomena are manifestations of the mind.

***Longchenpa*** (1308–1363), known as the "Great Omniscient One" and the "Second Garab Dorje," was a Dzogchen master admired by all schools of Tibetan Buddhism for the majestic scope of his Dzogchen and tantric writings, which reconciled and synthesized many prior traditions. His "Seven Treasuries" are a monument of Tibetan religious literature, and his more than 250 treatises on all manner of subjects have informed the doctrinal core of Nyingma monastic learning for five hundred years. It is widely held that no one in history has written on the Dzogchen view as powerfully and eloquently as he. Many masters have said that simply by reading Longchenpa's Dzogchen writings one will directly experience the Dzogchen state.

***Machik Labdron*** (1055–1143) was a student of Pa Dampa Sangye and the mother of the practice of Chöd, a radical synthesis of the Prajnaparamita tradition and tantric guru yoga that "cuts through" the ego.

***Madhyamaka***, or the Middle Way school, maintains that all phenomena are encompassed by the two truths, absolute and relative. All phenomena are considered illusory manifestations of the true nature. Even mind—the ground of consciousness—is devoid of substantial existence. The tenets of Madhyamaka are based mainly on the Prajnaparamita sutras.

***Mahamudra*** means "Great Seal." It is the most direct practice for realization of buddha-nature in Vajrayana practice, according to the New Translation schools of Tibetan Buddhism, which include Kagyu, Sakya, and Gelug.

***Mahaparinirvana*** is the final passing beyond suffering experienced by buddhas and highly realized masters at the end of their lives.

***Mahasiddha*** means "great accomplished one." It refers to a master of meditation, particularly one who is capable of great magical power.

***Mahayana*** literally means the "Greater Vehicle." The Mahayana teachings are characterized by the practice of the six paramitas and the cultivation of the altruistic intention to free all beings from the sufferings of samsara, thus leading them to complete enlightenment. The path practiced by bodhisattvas, the Mahayana emphasizes the recognition of the emptiness of both self and other. Both the sutras and tantras are included within this vehicle. See ***nine yanas***.

***Maitreya*** is the "buddha of the future," the fifth buddha of this Fortune Aeon, and the successor of Buddha Shakyamuni. *Maitreya* means "loving-kindness." It is also possible to interpret Maitreya as being one's own potential for enlightenment—the future buddha within oneself.

***Manjushri-nama-samgiti***, or *Chanting the Names of Manjushri*, is a renowned tantra that invokes the buddha Manjushri as the embodiment of all knowledge.

***Manjushrimitra*** was one of the greatest scholars and panditas of his day. When he heard of Garab Dorje's teachings that transcended effort and the laws of cause and effect, he deemed them heretical. He searched for Garab Dorje with the hope of engaging and defeating him in debate. Manjushrimitra lost the debate, became Garab Dorje's student, and studied with him for seventy-five years, becoming his principal disciple and spiritual heir. It was Manjushrimitra who divided the Dzogchen teachings into three sections: Mind, Space, and Essence Instruction. Upon attaining the transcendental wisdom rainbow body, he imparted his last testament, known as the "Six Meditation Experiences," to his principal disciple, Shri Singha:

> O son of good family, if you wish to experience the continuity of naked awareness,
>
> 1. Focus on absolute awareness as the object.
> 2. Press the points of the body.

3. Close the way of coming and going.
4. Focus on the target.
5. Rely on the unmoving.
6. Grasp the vast expanse.

*Marpa* (1012–1097) was the great Tibetan lay master who inherited Naropa's complete lineage and passed it on to Milarepa.

*Mindfulness* means "alertness," "recollection," "not forgetting," "attentiveness," and "presence of mind."

The *Mind Only school* was expounded most famously by the great Asanga and Vasubandhu. This philosophical school is one of the four major schools of Buddhist philosophy. It generally claims that buddha-nature is mind free from the duality of subject and object; in fact, the very nature of reality is held to be buddha mind. The Mind Only school identifies three characteristics of knowledge, or three natures: (1) "exaggeration" or "imputed phenomena"; (2) "power of others"; and (3) "absolute existence." According to Mind Only, absolute existence is the original nature, free from exaggeration. If we look closely at the things we label, we find that such things are not substantially existent; they have no independent, core existence. And who is it that perceives this exaggeration? It is none other than mind itself. None of the things we experience exist outside of mind, since everything we experience is labeled and reflected within mind. The "other power" of mind creates this exaggeration. But whether we are talking about the exaggeration itself or the other power of dualistic mind, upon close examination we find that neither is substantially existent. This lack of a core existence is not a newly developed concept but is actually inherent as our original nature. It is the way things originally are, the absolute nature of emptiness.

The *Mind Section of Dzogchen*, also known as *Mind Class*, or *Dzogchen Semde*, was the first of the three transmission lineages of Dzogchen, taught principally by Vairochana and Vimalamitra. By applying the instructions of the Mind Section, all phenomena that dualistically appear as subject and object are transcended. See *nine yanas*.

*Mitra Dzokyi*, also known as Mitra Yogi, was a twelfth-century siddha from India who received teachings from Avalokiteshvara. The transmission of Mitra Dzokyi's *Six Vajra Yogas* still exists. The text can be found in volume sixteen of Jamgon Kongtrul's *Treasury of Oral Instructions*.

*Nagarjuna* (50 B.C.E.–550 C.E.) was the first Madhyamaka teacher, born about four hundred years after the mahaparinirvana of Buddha Shakyamuni. He was the second head abbot of Nalanda Monastery, one of India's most renowned centers of Buddhist training and education, situated in the present state of Bihar. Guided by the bodhisattva Manjushri, Nagarjuna summarized the philosophy of the *Prajnaparamita* in a condensed way that is easy to follow. He wrote a very famous book called *Prajna-nama-mula-madhyamaka-karika*. In Tibetan, this work is known as *Uma Tsawai Sherab*, and it is sometimes translated into English as *Root Verses on Madhyamaka*. The *Mula-madhyamaka-karika* has twenty-seven chapters, but these chapters are not based on Nagarjuna's own presumptions; his work relies on logic, reason, and the reader's own intelligence to explore and introduce the nature as it is. Nagarjuna wrote four or five additional texts to further support and explain the root text of the *Mula-madhyamaka-karika*. These are called the *Six Treatises of the Reasoning of Madhyamaka*, and together they clearly establish the view of Madhyamaka.

***Naropa*** was the disciple of Tilopa and the teacher of Marpa. The endurance and devotion he demonstrated as he was tested and trained by Tilopa is legendary. He is famous for his Six Yogas. He is an archetype of the scholar who becomes a siddha by serving a guru. Tilopa's last words to him were, "Do not imagine, think, deliberate, or act, but be at rest. Have no concern for an object."

***Ngöndro***, or foundational practices, in Tibetan Buddhism embodies all the teachings of the Buddha. Ngöndro includes both "common" and "extraordinary" practices. The common ngöndro is composed of the four thoughts that turn the mind away from samsara, which include (1) contemplating the preciousness of human life, (2) the fragility of life and impermanent nature of all things, (3) practicing virtue and avoiding harmful actions, and (4) clearly seeing the inherent suffering of conditioned existence. The extraordinary ngöndro includes the practices of refuge and bodhichitta, Vajrasattva recitation, mandala offering, and guru yoga. These essential preliminary practices establish the foundation that prepares a student to receive additional Vajrayana teachings by purifying their obscurations, accumulating merit and wisdom, and receiving the blessings of the lineage masters.

The ***nine yanas*** comprise the complete Buddhist path according to the Nyingma school. They are enumerated as follows:

1. Shravakayana, or Hearer Vehicle
2. Pratyekabuddhayana, or Solitary Realizer Vehicle
3. Bodhisattvayana, or Bodhisattva Vehicle
4. Kriyayogatantra, or Action Yoga Tantra
5. Upayogatantra, or Dual Yoga Tantra
6. Yogayogatantra, or Yoga Tantra
7. Mahayogatantra, or Great Yoga Tantra
8. Anuyogatantra, or Subsequent Yoga Tantra
9. Atiyogatantra, or Supreme Yoga Tantra

According to the Nyingma classification, the first two yanas are known as "foundational Buddhism," or "Hinayana," and all the rest of the yanas—the third through the ninth—are known as "Mahayana." The Vajrayana, also known as "Tantrayana," includes everything from Kriyayoga (the fourth yana) up to and including Atiyoga (the ninth). Yanas four through six—Kriyayoga, Upayoga, and Yogayoga—comprise the outer tantras, while yanas seven through nine—Mahayoga, Anuyoga, and Atiyoga—make up the inner tantras.

***Nirmanakaya*** means "emanation body," which may refer to an incarnated bodhisattva who works for the welfare of sentient beings or the nirmanakaya emanation of a buddha. According to Dzogchen, nirmanakaya refers to the mind's constantly erupting, ceaseless play, or the constant flow of thoughts and emotions.

***Nonduality*** literally means "not two" and is the realization that in absolute truth, there is no "I" and no "other"; that all external phenomena are inseparable from mind, which itself is free from all grasping.

***Nyingma*** means "ancient tradition." The earliest of the four main schools of Tibetan Buddhism, it follows the teachings of Guru Padmasambhava, Shantarakshita, and Vimalamitra first propagated in Tibet in the eighth century during the reign of King Trisong Deutsen. The so-called New Translation schools of Tibetan Buddhism—Kadam, Kagyu, Sakya, and Gelug—are based primarily on translations of Dharma texts that were undertaken when a new wave of Buddhist teachings came from India during the eleventh century. It was after this point that the lineage associated with the early dissemination of Buddhism in Tibet came to be known as "Ancient."

The ***outer tantras*** include Kriyatantra, Upatantra, and Yogatantra according to the nine-yana system of the Nyingma school. While viewing everything without exception as a display of emptiness, one performs outer purification practices of body and speech, and connects one's mind to an already fully enlightened being, thereby receiving their blessings and becoming a buddha oneself. See ***nine yanas***.

***Pa Dampa Sangye*** (eleventh century) was an Indian mahasiddha who visited Tibet at least three times before eventually settling in Tingri. He is the father of Chöd, and his best-known teaching is Pacification (pronounced *zhijé*), referring to the pacification of suffering. His testament to the people of Tingri, called the *Hundred Verses of Advice*, contains one hundred epigrams that encompass the entire Buddhist path. It has been renowned and studied for centuries.

***Paramita*** literally means "reaching the other shore." In particular, this term refers to engaging in altruistic activities motivated by the wish to achieve enlightenment for all sentient beings, carried out in conjunction with the other paramitas and with awareness of emptiness that transcends the concepts of subject, object, and action. One practices the six paramitas according to the Mahayana and Vajrayana instructions, thus accumulating wisdom and merit that will lead to the far shore of enlightenment. The six paramitas are (1) generosity, (2) morality, (3) patience, (4) joyful effort, (5) concentration, and (6) discriminating wisdom.

***Patrul Rinpoche*** (1808–1887), a great Nyingma master, was well known as a scholar, poet, and teacher. His powerful teachings were very direct and able to uproot and eliminate the errors of practitioners. He wandered from village to village, gathering the population and practicing Avalokiteshvara and Amitabha with them. He promoted peace, love, and harmony among everyone, and encouraged them to refrain from the slaughter and hunting of animals. Though he was the teacher of so many great disciples, he remained a humble and simple wandering hermitage monk.

***Prajnaparamita*** literally means "transcendent wisdom." The Prajnaparamita sutras contain the Mahayana teachings on emptiness associated with the second turning of the wheel of Dharma, which explain how to transcend fixation on subject, object, and action.

***Relative truth*** refers to ordinary, habitual, conditioned beliefs—unique to one person or shared collectively—about how the world is.

***Rigpa*** is the bright and open intelligence, ungoverned by thoughts and emotions, inherent within all sentient beings. It is often translated as "awareness."

***Rongzom Chokyi Zangpo***, or Rongzompa (1012–1131), was a great Nyingma kama master whom Atisha recognized as the incarnation of the Indian master Nagpo Chopa. He was considered to be the immediate reincarnation of two other Indian masters: Smriti Jnana Kirti and Trala Ringmo. He was a master of many languages, including those of the animals. A great scholar, he wrote a renowned commentary on the *Guhyagarbha Tantra*, and many other philosophical works, as well as books on animal husbandry, agriculture, and dairy farming. Rongzompa is renowned as being one of the "two eyes" of the Nyingma tradition; the other is Longchenpa.

***Samadhi***. See ***shamatha***.

***Sambhogakaya*** means the "buddha body of complete enjoyment" directly experienced by high-level bodhisattvas. According to Dzogchen, sambhogakaya is the knowing capacity of mind, or the energy, clarity, and vitality of our innate awareness of dharmakaya. It is the spontaneously accomplished and inherent richness of wisdom.

***Sangye Yeshe*** (ninth and tenth centuries) was one of the twenty-five disciples of Guru Padmasambhava as well as a disciple of Shantarakshita and Vimalamitra. He was the second great native-Tibetan lineage holder of the Nyingma kama teachings. He was the chief exponent of the Anuyoga tantras in Tibet and was renowned as an unequaled master of magical power as well as being the "Lord of the Ngakpas." He was a great scholar, writing about five treatises, including *Lamp for the Eye of Meditation*. He translated over twenty-six inner tantras related to Yamantaka, the wrathful form of Manjushri.

The ***seven-line prayer*** is the greatest and most powerful of all supplications to Guru Padmasambhava. It is chanted as a declaration of faith and devotion to one's spiritual master and as a reminder to abide in the nature of the mind. As the great master Mipham Rinpoche taught in the *White Lotus*, the seven-line prayer encompasses every aspect of the Buddhadharma, particularly the inner tantras.

***Shamatha*** is made of two words, *shama* and *tha*. *Shama* means "peaceful or calm," and *tha* means "letting or abiding," so shamatha means "letting the mind be peaceful." Shamatha is also known in Sanskrit as *samadhi*, which is also two words put together. *Sama* means "motionless" and *dhi* means "holding," so samadhi refers to maintaining one's mind in a constant, unchanging state. When your mind rests single-pointedly, undisturbed by thoughts, it becomes calm.

***Shantarakshita***, considered to be an emanation of Vajrapani, was the head abbot of Nalanda monastic university. He was a renowned logician and philosopher who composed the *Ornament of the Middle Way*, which became the basis of the Yogachara-Madhyamaka philosophical school by combining the Mind Only and Madhyamaka schools. In the eighth century, King Trisong Deutsen invited him to Tibet in order to establish Buddhism there. When they met, Shantarakshita took the young king's hand and asked him if he remembered their past-life pledge. Shantarakshita told King Trisong Deutsen how he had stayed in the world for nine generations waiting for him to take birth. He was the cofounder of Tibetan Buddhism, and ordained the first seven monks in Tibet. He taught both the sutras and tantras to many disciples and trained the first Tibetan translators, as well as translating many texts himself. Several of the original twenty-five disciples of Guru Padmasambhava were also his students. He was renowned for his kindness and gentleness. In Tibet, he is known as Khenchen Bodhisattva.

***Shedra*** is the philosophical training of systematically listening to and contemplating the teachings of the Buddha in order to fully absorb their meaning into your heart and mind with the practice of meditation.

***Shri Singha***, heeding prophecies made by Avalokiteshvara, went to Manjushrimitra and studied with him for twenty-five years, becoming his principal disciple. Shri Singha received Manjushrimitra's last testament, the *Six Meditation Experiences*, as Manjushrimitra entered mahaparinirvana. Shri Singha thus became the third lineage holder of the complete Dzogchen teachings and later became the first to spread them more widely. When he attained the transcendental wisdom rainbow body, he imparted his last testament to Jnanasutra, known as the *Seven Nails:*

> Homage to perfect primordial wisdom, the unity of clarity and emptiness, the great self-existing awareness, open and impartial, which pervades and abides in all. Nail the original, unchanging round with the seven great nails of the path of nonduality, and unchanging great bliss will arise.
>
> 1. Nail samsara and nirvana together with the unobstructed clarity of pure wisdom.
> 2. Nail the observer and the observed together with the self-appearing clear light.
> 3. Nail mind and matter together with the spontaneous pure essence.
> 4. Nail phenomena and the nature of phenomena together with absolute awareness.
> 5. Nail nihilism and eternalism together with freedom from views.
> 6. Nail elation and depression together with the liberation of the sense faculties.
> 7. Nail appearances and emptiness together with the primordially perfect dharmakaya.

***Skillful means practices*** are the varieties of techniques used to quickly develop wisdom and help free all sentient beings from suffering. By strongly connecting to love, compassion, devotion, and all the positive qualities of mind, the conceptual and emotional obscurations that temporarily block our wisdom are quickly dissolved, and the beneficial effects of our practice are multiplied enormously.

The ***Space Instruction Section*** is one of the three transmission lineages of Dzogchen and was taught primarily by Vairochana. According to these instructions, all conditioned phenomena that appear are the ornaments of self-born wisdom. Applying these teachings establishes the infinity of primordial liberation without using any analysis. See ***nine yanas***.

***Superior insight***. See ***vipashyana***.

***Sutras*** are the original discourses given by Buddha Shakyamuni to his disciples. A sutra always begins with the statement "Thus I have heard," followed by details of the time and place at which the sutra was taught, the students' questions and the Buddha's answers, and concludes with everyone rejoicing in the teachings. These discourses were compiled and transcribed by his arhat followers at a gathering held shortly after the Awakened One's mahaparinirvana. ***Sutra*** can also refer to the second of the Three Baskets.

***Sutrayana***. The general distinction between the visions of the Sutrayana and the Vajrayana is related to their "causal" and "resultant" views. The Sutrayana is often referred to as the "causal yana." In these teachings one gathers good foundations and causes, and results gradually begin to sprout based on the accumulation of these causes. In contrast, in the Vajrayana, known as the "resultant yana," or "effect yana," one instantly approaches the enlightened qualities of one's buddhanature without gradually gathering the causes and conditions. The Vajrayana immediately jumps to that state, instantly discovering the resultant vision of pure body, speech, and mind. The Sutrayana includes (1) the Shravakayana, (2) the Pratyekabuddhayana, and (3) the Bodhisattvayana. See ***nine yanas***.

***Terma*** are Dharma treasures of texts and relics hidden throughout Tibet, Nepal, Bhutan, and elsewhere in the eighth and ninth centuries by Guru Padmasambhava with the assistance of Yeshe Tsogyal. These treasures are later discovered at the appropriate time by destined disciples.

***Tertons***, or treasure revealers, recover the hidden terma treasures from the earth and the sky, as pure visions, and even from their own minds, where they were concealed.

The ***Three Roots*** are the lama; yidam, or tutelary deity; and khandro. They are the sources of blessings, accomplishment, and action, respectively. The teachings of Guru Padmasambhava often refer to the Three Roots as the inner refuge, while the outer refuge is the Three Jewels of the Buddha, Dharma, and Sangha.

The ***three vows*** refers to the pratimoksha, or individual liberation, vow; the bodhisattva vow; and the Vajrayana vow. These are explained as follows:

1. To achieve spiritual liberation for oneself, to harm no one, and to practice good conduct in the world. If one is ordained, it means to follow the Vinaya. This is the pratimoksha vow.
2. To treat all others with loving-kindness and compassion, and to guide them

to spiritual liberation skillfully and according to their needs. This is the bodhisattva vow.

3. To see the universe and everything within it as pure and perfect. This is the Vajrayana vow.

***Tilopa*** is the father of the Kagyu lineage. He is most famous as the powerful and enigmatic guru of Naropa. His songs are essential Mahamudra teachings.

***Tögal*** is one of the two main Dzogchen practices; it literally means the "leap-over that puts one on top." The practice of tögal unveils the radiance, clarity, and power of the nature of the mind; it also reveals the essences of the five elements—space, wind, fire, water, and earth—that comprise the physical universe. A good foundation in trekchö is needed for the practice of tögal to fully blossom.

The ***transcendental wisdom rainbow body*** is the transformation of the gross physical body into a body of pure light that can occur at the time of death for advanced Dzogchen practitioners, if they so choose.

***Trekchö*** literally means "cutting through." It is the path of effortlessly letting go of all subjective interference; it is opening oneself up to pure experience that is absolutely ungoverned by ideas and emotions. Trekchö is the foundation practice of Dzogchen; it reveals the vast expanse of the dharmakaya, while tögal reveals the full splendor of the sambhogakaya and nirmanakaya.

The ***twelve Dzogchen buddhas***, also known as the twelve Dzogchen teachers, are emanations of the primordial buddha Samantabhadra who lived in ancient times. They are the progenitors of Dzogchen.

The ***Uttaratantra*** is a commentary on the Buddha's teachings on buddha-nature, which is the potential for enlightenment inherent in every living being, taught by the future buddha Maitreya and the great scholar and siddha Asanga.

The ***Vajra Guru mantra*** is the sound-essence of Guru Padmasambhava, and the entire path of the Buddhadharma in twelve sacred syllables.

***Vajrayana*** is also known as the "Adamantine Vehicle," "Indestructible Vehicle," "Secret Mantrayana," and "Mantrayana." The latter two names indicate that mind is protected from dualistic conceptions through the practice of this vehicle. In the Sanskrit word *mantra*, the root *mana* can be translated as "mind" and the suffix *tra* can be translated as "protection." On one level, the Vajrayana is referred to as "secret" because it has traditionally been transmitted from a qualified teacher to a qualified disciple and kept hidden from those who would misinterpret the teachings and thereby harm themselves and others. However, on a deeper level, this secret quality alludes to the "self-secret" nature of awareness that remains hidden from dualistic mind. There are two very important foundational elements to all Vajrayana practice: (1) a vast and sincere motivation of bodhichitta, which is the strong wish to bring all sentient beings, without partiality, to the state of complete enlightenment; and (2) a pure understanding or view that regards all phenomena—including one's own aggregates—as the pervasive wisdom display of the "three vajra states," the inseparable union of wisdom and compassion. See ***nine yanas***.

***Vimalamitra*** was one of the greatest Indian Buddhist scholars and siddhas, and one of the masters and originators of Dzogchen in Tibet, along with Guru Padmasambhava and Vairochana. He came to Tibet in the eighth century and stayed for about twelve years. He left the country for seven years, and then at the royal request of King Mune Tsenpo returned for a brief period. He taught and translated into Tibetan numerous sutras and tantras. His essential teaching is called the *Vima Nyingtik*, or the *Heart Essence of Vimalamitra*. He achieved the transcendental wisdom rainbow body and is said to be residing in that form at the Five-Peaked Mountain in China. According to the teachings, an emanation of Vimalamitra appears every century in the human world in order to revitalize the Dzogchen teachings.

The ***Vinaya*** is the first of the Three Baskets; it includes the Buddha's teachings on ethics in general and on monastic discipline in particular. The Vinaya is founded on the pratimoksha, or individual liberation, vows.

***Vipashyana*** is insight meditation, or the open quality of awareness that penetrates the nature of its selected object. On the ultimate level, Vipashyana refers to resting in the transparent, lucid state of the true nature, free from conceptual thoughts or elaboration. After having developed one-pointed concentration through shamatha meditation, one infuses that concentration with penetrating insight into the nature of reality. Dzogchen is the union of absolute shamatha and absolute vipashyana.

***Yangönpa*** (1213–1287) was one of the great masters of the Drukpa Kagyu school and a principal disciple of Götsangpa.

***Yeshe Tsogyal*** is considered an emanation of both Saraswati, the buddha of wisdom and arts, and Tara, the female buddha of compassion. At a very early age, she was King Trisong Deutsen's queen. Later, King Trisong Deutsen offered his entire kingdom and all that he held most precious to Guru Padmasambhava, and she became Padmasambhava's spiritual consort and his chief Tibetan female disciple, receiving all the transmissions he gave in Tibet. She is renowned for her photographic memory. She later compiled all his teachings, recording them in symbolic dakini language and script. In this way, she and Guru Padmasambhava hid these terma teachings throughout Tibet and in bordering countries to be discovered at various times in the future by great tertons. After living for more than two hundred years and having attained the transcendental wisdom rainbow body through her practice of Dzogchen meditation, she went to Glorious Copper-Colored Mountain—the pure land of Guru Padmasambhava—without leaving any physical remains behind.

***Zen*** is a form of Mahayana Buddhism in which sitting meditation, koan study, and the relationship between master and disciple are the primary means for spiritual awakening.

# Illustration Credits

*Dedication page:* His Holiness Dudjom Rinpoche: photographer unknown. Khenchen Palden Sherab Rinpoche, West Palm Beach, Florida, 2008: photograph by Derek Sarno. Lama Chimed Namgyal, West Palm Beach, Florida, 1994: photograph by Mimi Bailey.

*page 38:* Guru Padmasambhava and Yeshe Tsogyal. Personal thangka of the Khenpo Rinpoches.

*page 51:* Patrul Rinpoche. Mural painting at Padma Samye Ling Temple.

*page 66:* Self-Awareness. Calligraphy by Khenpo Tsewang Dongyal Rinpoche.

*page 79:* Originally Liberated into Vast Space. Calligraphy by Khenpo Tsewang Dongyal Rinpoche.

*page 93:* Self-Clarity of Mindfulness. Calligraphy by Khenpo Tsewang Dongyal Rinpoche.

*page 98:* Semde, Longde, and Mennagde. Calligraphy by Khenpo Tsewang Dongyal Rinpoche.

*page 112:* Shantideva. Mural painting at Padma Samye Ling Temple.

*page 126:* Longchenpa. Mural painting at Padma Samye Ling Temple.

*page 159:* Bodhichitta Is the Core of the Buddha's Teachings. Calligraphy by Khenpo Tsewang Dongyal Rinpoche.

*page 191:* Dharma Protectors Mahakala, Ekajati, Dorje Lekpa, and Rahula. Mural paintings at Padma Samye Ling Temple.

# About the Authors

## Khenchen Palden Sherab Rinpoche (1938–2010)

Venerable Khenchen Palden Sherab Rinpoche was a renowned scholar and meditation master of the Nyingma school of Tibetan Buddhism. He was born on May 10, 1938, in the Dhoshul region of Kham in eastern Tibet, near the sacred mountain Jowo Zegyal. On the morning of his birth, a small snow fell with flakes in the shape of lotus petals. Among his ancestors were many great scholars, practitioners, and tertons.

His family was seminomadic, living in the village during the winter and moving with the herds to high mountain pastures in the summer, where they lived in yak-hair tents. The monastery for the Dhoshul region, founded by the great terton Tsasum Lingpa, is known as Gochen Monastery, and his father's family had the hereditary responsibility for administration of the business affairs of the monastery. His grandfather had been both administrator and chant master in charge of the ritual ceremonies.

Khenchen Rinpoche began his education at Gochen Monastery at age four. He entered Riwoche Monastery at age fourteen, completing his studies there just before the Chinese invasion of Tibet reached the area. Among his root teachers was the illustrious Khenchen Tenzin Dragpa (Katok Khenpo Akshu).

In 1959, Khenchen Rinpoche and his family were forced into exile, escaping to India. After the tumultuous period following their escape, in 1967 he was appointed head of the Nyingma department of the Central Institute of Higher Tibetan Studies in Sarnath by His Holiness Dudjom Rinpoche, the Supreme Head of the Nyingma school of Tibetan Buddhism. He held this position of abbot for seventeen years, dedicating all his time and energy to ensure the survival and spread of the Buddha's teachings. Venerable Khenchen Palden Sherab Rinpoche moved to the United States in 1984 to work closely with His Holiness Dudjom Rinpoche. In 1985, he and his brother, Venerable Khenpo Tsewang Dongyal Rinpoche, founded the Dharma Samudra Publishing Company. In 1988, they founded the Padmasambhava Buddhist Center (PBC), which has centers throughout the United States as well as in Puerto Rico, Russia, and India, among other countries. The principal center is Palden Padma Samye Ling, located in Delaware County in upstate New York. PBC also includes a traditional Tibetan Buddhist monastery and nunnery at the holy site of Deer Park in Sarnath, and the Miracle Stupa for World Peace at Padma Samye Jetavan, which is in Jetavan Grove, Shravasti, India.

Khenchen Palden Sherab Rinpoche traveled extensively within the United States and throughout the world, giving teachings and empowerments, conducting retreats and seminars, and establishing meditation centers. He authored three volumes of Tibetan works, and coauthored over twenty-five books in English with Venerable Khenpo Tsewang Dongyal Rinpoche. His collected Tibetan works include:

*Opening the Eyes of Wisdom*, a commentary on Sangye Yeshe's *Lamp of the Eye of Contemplation*
*Waves of the Ocean of Devotion*, a biography-praise to Nubchen Sangye Yeshe, and *Vajra Rosary*, biographies of his main incarnations
*The Mirror of Mindfulness*, an explanation of the six bardos
*Advice from the Ancestral Vidyadhara*, a commentary on Padmasambhava's *Stages of the Path, Heap of Jewels*
*Blazing Clouds of Wisdom and Compassion*, a commentary on the hundred-syllable mantra of Vajrasattva
*The Ornament of Vairochana's Intention*, a commentary on the *Heart Sutra*
*Opening the Door of Blessings*, a biography of Machik Labdron
*Lotus Necklace of Devotion*, a biography of Khenchen Tenzin Dragpa
*The Essence of Diamond Clear Light*, an outline and structural analysis of *The Aspiration Prayer of Samantabhadra*
*The Lamp of Blazing Sun and Moon*, a commentary on Mipham Rinpoche's *Wisdom Sword*
*The Ornament of Stars at Dawn*, an outline and structural analysis of Vasubandhu's *Twenty Verses*
*Pleasure Lake of Nagarjuna's Intention*, a general summary of Madhyamaka
*Supreme Clear Mirror*, an introduction to Buddhist logic
*White Lotus*, an explanation of prayers to Guru Rinpoche
*Smiling Red Lotus*, a short commentary on the prayer to Yeshe Tsogyal
*Clouds of Blessings*, an explanation of prayers to Terchen Tsasum Lingpa, and other learned works, poems, prayers and sadhanas
*The Smile of Sun and Moon:* A Commentary on the *Praise to the Twenty-One Taras*

## Khenpo Tsewang Dongyal Rinpoche

Venerable Khenpo Tsewang Dongyal Rinpoche was born in the Dhoshul region of Kham in eastern Tibet, on June 10, 1950. On that summer day in the family tent, Khenpo Rinpoche's birth caused his mother, Pema Lhadze, no pain. The next day, upon moving the bed where she had delivered the baby, his mother found growing a beautiful and fragrant flower, which she plucked and offered to Chenrezig on the family altar. Soon after Khenpo Tsewang was born, three head lamas from Jadchag Monastery came to his home and recognized him as the reincarnation of Khenpo Sherab Khyentse, who had been the former head abbot at Gochen Monastery. Sherab Khyentse was a renowned scholar and practitioner who spent much of his life in retreat.

Khenpo Rinpoche began his formal schooling at age five, when he entered Gochen Monastery. However, his first Dharma teacher was his father, Lama Chimed Namgyal Rinpoche. The Chinese invasion of Tibet interrupted his studies, and he escaped to India with his family in 1959. There his father and brother continued his education until he entered the Nyingmapa Monastic School of northern India, where he studied until 1967. Khenpo Rinpoche then entered the Central Institute of Higher Tibetan Studies, which at the time was part of Sanskrit University in Varanasi, where he received his BA degree in 1975. He also attended Nyingmapa University in West Bengal, where he received another BA and an MA in 1977.

In 1978, His Holiness Dudjom Rinpoche enthroned Venerable Khenpo Tsewang Dongyal Rinpoche as the abbot of the Wish-fulfilling Nyingmapa Institute in Boudhanath, Nepal, where he taught poetry, grammar, and philosophy. Then, in 1981, His Holiness appointed Khenpo Rinpoche as the abbot of the Dorje Nyingpo center in Paris, France. Finally, in 1982, he asked Khenpo Tsewang to work with him at the Yeshe Nyingpo center in New York. From that time until His Holiness Dudjom Rinpoche's mahaparinirvana in 1987, Khenpo Rinpoche continued to work closely with him, often traveling with His Holiness as his translator and attendant.

In 1988, Khenpo Tsewang Dongyal Rinpoche and his brother, Venerable Khenchen Palden Sherab Rinpoche, founded the Padmasambhava Buddhist Center. Since that time, he has served as a spiritual director at the various Padmasambhava Buddhist Centers throughout the world. He maintains an active traveling and teaching schedule.

Khenpo Rinpoche is the author of *Light of Fearless Indestructible Wisdom: The Life and Legacy of His Holiness Dudjom Rinpoche*, published in both Tibetan and English. He has also authored a book of poetry on the life of Guru Rinpoche entitled *Praise to the Lotus Born: A Verse Garland of Waves of Devotion*, and a unique two-volume cultural and religious history of Tibet entitled *Six Sublime Pillars of the Nyingma School*, which details the historical bases of the Dharma in Tibet from the sixth to ninth centuries. At present, *Six Sublime Pillars* is one of the only books to convey the Dharma activities of this period in such depth, and His Holiness Dudjom Rinpoche encouraged Khenpo Tsewang to complete it, describing the work as an important contribution to the history of the kama lineage.

Along with these, Khenpo Tsewang Dongyal Rinpoche has coauthored over twenty-five Dharma books in English with Venerable Khenchen Palden Sherab Rinpoche.

## Other Works by the Authors

### *Padma Samye Ling Shedra Series*

The Venerable Khenpo Rinpoches have taught the Dharma in the United States for more than thirty years. In that time, they have given over a decade of shedra teachings. These clear and profound teachings include detailed summaries and commentaries by great Nyingma masters such as Kunkhyen Longchenpa and Mipham Rinpoche. Each of the PSL Shedra Series books distills the essential meaning of the Nyingmapa shedra program that the Venerable Rinpoches received in Tibet as the last generation of lamas to be taught in the traditional monastic setting, which had carefully preserved the lineage teachings for centuries.

The PSL Shedra Series currently includes the following titles:

1. *Opening the Clear Vision of the Vaibhashika and Sautrantika Schools*
2. *Opening the Clear Vision of the Mind Only School*
3. *Opening the Wisdom Door of the Madhyamaka School*
4. *Opening the Wisdom Door of the Rangtong and Shentong Views: A Brief Explanation of the One Taste of the Second and Third Turning of the Wheel of Dharma*
5. *Opening the Wisdom Door of the Outer Tantras: Refining Awareness Through Ascetic Ritual and Purification Practice*
6. *Turning the Wisdom Wheel of the Nine Golden Chariots*
7. *Splendid Presence of the Great Guhyagarbha: Opening the Wisdom Door of the King of All Tantras*
8. *Key to Opening the Wisdom Door of Anuyoga: Exploring the One Taste of the Three Mandalas*

### *Opening the Door of the Dharma Treasury Practice Guides*

A series of condensed instructions on some of the main practices of the Padmasambhava Buddhist Center and Nyingma lineage:

1. *Practice Guide for a Eulogy Praising the Twelve Deeds in the Life of Lord Buddha*
2. *Commentary on the Blessing Treasure: A Sadhana of the Buddha Shakyamuni*
3. *Practice Guide of the Seven Line Prayer of Padmasambhava*
4. *Practice Guide for the Contemplation of the Four Thoughts That Turn the Mind from Samsara*
5. *Practice Guide for the Contemplation of Vows and Conduct in the Nyingma Tradition*

***Other Publications***

*The Beauty of Awakened Mind: Dzogchen Lineage of the Great Master Shigpo Dudtsi*
*The Buddhist Path: A Practical Guide from the Nyingma Tradition of Tibetan Buddhism* (formerly entitled *Opening to Our Primordial Nature* and *Light of the Three Jewels*)
*Ceaseless Echoes of the Great Silence: A Commentary on the Heart Sutra Prajnaparamita*
*The Dark Red Amulet: Oral Instructions on the Practice of Vajrakilaya*
*Discovering Infinite Freedom: The Prayer of Küntuzangpo*
*Door to Inconceivable Wisdom and Compassion*
*The Essential Journey of Life and Death*
*Volume 1: Indestructible Nature of Body, Speech, and Mind*
*Volume 2: Using Dream Yoga and Phowa as the Path*
*Heart Essence of Chetsun: Voice of the Lion* (restricted)
*Illuminating the Path: Ngondro Instructions according to the Nyingma School of Vajrayana Buddhism*
*Liberating Duality with Wisdom Display: The Eight Emanations of Guru Padmasambhava*
*Light of Fearless Indestructible Wisdom: The Life and Legacy of His Holiness Dudjom Rinpoche*
*Lion's Gaze: A Commentary on the Tsig Sum Nedek*
*Praise to the Lotus Born: A Verse Garland of Waves of Devotion*
*Prajñaparamita: The Six Perfections*
*The Smile of Sun and Moon: A Commentary on the Praise to the Twenty-One Taras*
*Supreme Wisdom: Commentary on Yeshe Lama* (restricted)
*Tara's Enlightened Activity*

## Padmasambhava Buddhist Center

Venerable Khenchen Palden Sherab Rinpoche and Venerable Khenpo Tsewang Dongyal Rinpoche established the Padmasambhava Buddhist Center (PBC) to preserve the authentic message of Buddha Shakyamuni and Guru Padmasambhava in its entirety, and in particular to teach the tradition of Nyingmapa and Vajrayana Buddhism. It is dedicated to world peace and the supreme good fortune and well-being of all. PBC now includes over twenty centers in the United States, Russia, Canada, and Puerto Rico, in addition to monastic institutions in India, Russia, and the United States.

The Samye Translation Group was founded by the Venerable Khenpo Rinpoches to commemorate and preserve the great ancient tradition of translation that was firmly established during the glorious Tibetan Buddhist era of the seventh through tenth centuries. As a reflection of gratitude for the unique activities of these enlightened translators, the Samye Translation Group has published Dharma books that cover all nine yana teachings of the Nyingma school of Tibetan Buddhism, including shedra philosophy books.

For more information about the Venerable Khenpo Rinpoches' activities, the Samye Translation Group, or Padmasambhava Buddhist Center, please contact:

Padma Samye Ling
618 Buddha Highway
Sidney Center, NY 13839
(607) 865-8068
www.padmasambhava.org

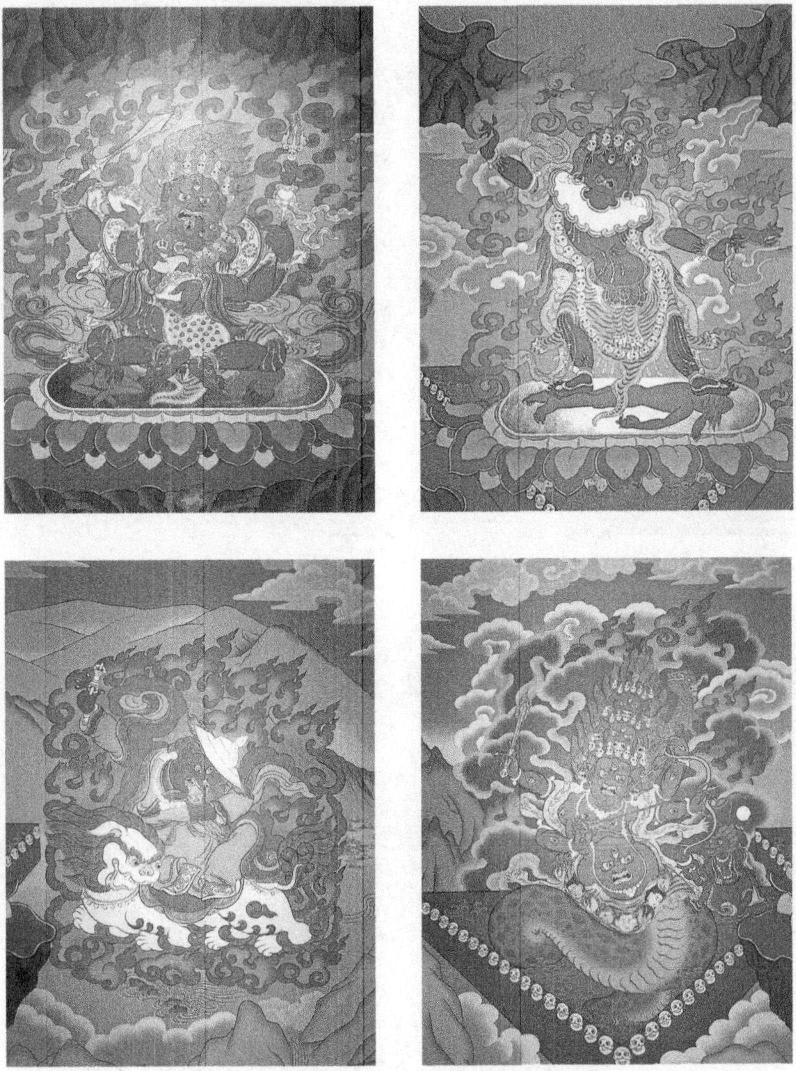

Dharma Protectors Mahakala, Ekajati,
Dorje Lekpa, and Rahula